GW01157888

Education ⟶ be clear. Is it formalized education?

Relative

Subordinate party

Revocable Trusts Line by Line

A Detailed Look at Revocable Trusts and How to Adapt Them to Meet Your Needs

Kelley Galica Peck

ASPATORE

Mat #40788357

Copyright © 2008 by Thomson Reuters/Aspatore
All rights reserved. Printed in the United States of America.

Managing Editor, Sarah Gagnon; edited by Eddie Fournier; proofread by Melanie Zimmerman

No part of this publication may be reproduced or distributed in any form or by any means, or stored in a database or retrieval system, except as permitted under Sections 107 or 108 of the U.S. Copyright Act, without prior written permission of the publisher. This book is printed on acid-free paper.

Material in this book is for educational purposes only. This book is sold with the understanding that neither any of the authors nor the publisher are engaged in rendering legal, accounting, investment, or any other professional service. Neither the publisher nor the authors assume any liability for any errors or omissions, or for how this book or its contents are used or interpreted, or for any consequences resulting directly or indirectly from the use of this book. For legal advice or any other, please consult your personal lawyer or the appropriate professional.

The views expressed by the individuals in this book (or the individuals on the cover) do not necessarily reflect the views shared by the companies they are employed by (or the companies mentioned in this book). The employment status and affiliations of authors with the companies referenced are subject to change.

Aspatore books may be purchased for educational, business, or sales promotional use. For information, please e-mail West.customer.service@thomson.com.

ISBN 978-0-314-19459-6

For corrections, updates, comments, or any other inquiries, please e-mail TLR.AspatoreEditorial@thomson.com.

First Printing, 2008
10 9 8 7 6 5 4 3 2 1

ASPATORE

Aspatore Books, a Thomson Reuters business, is the largest and most exclusive publisher of C-level executives (CEO, CFO, CTO, CMO, partner) from the world's most respected companies and law firms. Aspatore annually publishes a select group of C-level executives from the Global 1,000, top 250 law firms (partners and chairs), and other leading companies of all sizes. C-Level Business Intelligence™, as conceptualized and developed by Aspatore Books, provides professionals of all levels with proven business intelligence from industry insiders—direct and unfiltered insight from those who know it best—as opposed to third-party accounts offered by unknown authors and analysts. Aspatore Books is committed to publishing an innovative line of business and legal books, those which lay forth principles and offer insights that, when employed, can have a direct financial impact on the reader's business objectives, whatever they may be. In essence, Aspatore publishes critical tools—need-to-read as opposed to nice-to-read books—for all business professionals.

CONTENTS

INTRODUCTION 9

LINE-BY-LINE ANALYSIS 21

APPENDIX A: THE FULL TRUST AGREEMENT 161

APPENDIX B: SOME ADDITIONAL CLAUSES 191

ABOUT THE AUTHOR 195

DEDICATION

*To Keith, Ian, and Brianna,
for the hours not spent at the park.*

Introduction

Revocable trusts have become an integral part of a well-developed estate plan. The revocable trust is essentially a "testamentary substitute," so called because it effectively provides for the disposition of an estate at death without the need for a will or probate of the decedent's assets. There are many other reasons why one might create a revocable trust, but the uses and benefits of those trusts are beyond the scope of this book.[1]

A revocable trust designed to serve as a testamentary substitute is usually referred to as a living trust, because it is designed to hold assets while the grantor is still living.[2] The individual who establishes the trust, generally referred to as the grantor, typically will be a trustee of the revocable living trust and is a beneficiary of the trust. In his or her capacity as trustee and beneficiary, the grantor retains control over the management and disposition of the assets. He or she can manage the investments, buy and sell assets, give away assets, and take property out of the trust at any time. However, because the property is legally owned by the trust and not the grantor, when the grantor dies, the assets of the trust are not subject to probate. Rather, the assets pass pursuant to the terms of the trust agreement.

---

[1] In addition to revocable trusts, there also are a wide variety of irrevocable trusts. There are significant differences between revocable and irrevocable trusts. Actually, that isn't true. The only real difference is that one can be revoked and the other cannot. Nonetheless, the practical effect in terms of the rules of property and tax law are dramatically different. This book does not address any of the irrevocable trusts or the legal issues surrounding them.

[2] Sometimes revocable living trusts are referred to as *inter vivos* trusts. While it is correct to say that a revocable living trust is an *inter vivos* trust, it is not an entirely adequate description. The term, from Latin, literally means "between the living" and is used in the legal sense to refer to any trust, revocable or irrevocable, created while the grantor is still alive. The term is used to distinguish such lifetime trusts from those that are established under a will that do not come into effect until the testator dies, referred to as "testamentary trusts." Thus, while all revocable living trusts are *inter vivos* trusts, not all *inter vivos* trusts are revocable living trusts.

A Word about Probate

Probate is a court-supervised system for the disposition of property at death. The probate system is necessary to ensure that property passes to the proper person at the death of the owner based on the decedent's will or, in the absence of a will, the laws of intestacy. Thus, probate of assets is necessary only when there is no other mechanism for the lawful transfer of property. There are a variety of mechanisms developed over the years to avoid probate. If property is owned by two or more individuals "with rights of survivorship," the property is not subject to probate when one of the co-owners dies.[3] Rather, the property passes automatically to the co-owner by operation of law. The use of a beneficiary designation to identify the successor owner for assets such as life insurance, transfer on death accounts (for both cash accounts and securities accounts), and retirement accounts is another popular means of avoiding probate. These alternate forms of ownership do accomplish the goal of avoiding probate. They do not, however, give the owner a significant degree of control over how the property will be received or when.

If an individual's sole objective is to avoid probate, joint ownership or beneficiary designation may be adequate to meet that goal. However, joint ownership with one heir will effectively disinherit all other heirs. The grantor also loses control over the assets when joint ownership is employed. With respect to bank and brokerage accounts, the joint owner has immediate access to the property and can withdraw the funds at any time. With jointly owned real estate, neither owner can sell without the consent of the other, absent expensive court proceedings to partition the property. Jointly held assets also are available to satisfy the creditors of the joint owners. Pay-on-death or beneficiary designations are less risky during the life of the owner, because the beneficiary has no access to or control over

---

[3] If property is owned by two or more individuals as "tenants-in-common," the property does not pass automatically by right of survivorship to the surviving joint tenants at death. Rather, the interest of the deceased joint tenant passes according to his or her will (or by intestacy if there is no will). The tenant-in-common interest is treated the same as sole ownership. When adopting a form of joint ownership for estate planning purposes, it is important to determine whether survivorship provisions are desirable and adopt the correct form of ownership. In many cases, failure to specify that ownership is intended to be with survivorship will result in the property being held as tenants-in-common. Some states allow a form of ownership known as "tenants-by-the-entirety," which is similar to joint ownership with rights of survivorship and is available only between spouses.

the property while the owner is living. However, the transfer by beneficiary designation, as with the transfer of joint ownership with rights of survivorship, is an absolute, outright transfer with no strings attached.

By contrast, use of a trust allows the <u>owner to place effective limitations</u> on <u>the time and</u> manner of <u>distribution of his or her property</u> to his or her heirs. Assets owned by a revocable trust are not subject to probate. They are not "owned" by the grantor, even if the grantor is the trustee. Rather, all assets owned by the trust pass according to the terms of the trust instrument. The grantor, by the terms of the instrument, can control when and how the assets will pass after his or her death. The use of a revocable trust is usually the superior means of avoiding probate if there are multiple heirs, if there is a risk associated with lifetime transfers to the beneficiaries, and if there is a desire to provide for post-death limitations on the timing or manner of transfer of assets. *Avoids death taxes*.

Of course, the use of a will can accomplish all of the same things that a revocable trust can accomplish, often at a lower cost, except to avoid the probate process. Why, then, is it so important to avoid probate? A great deal of myth and misunderstanding has grown up around the notion of avoiding probate. Most of the misinformation has been fueled by those in the industry of creating and selling books about "avoiding probate" and pre-packaged revocable trust documents. Certainly, some attorneys selling revocable trusts have also contributed to the notion that probate is to be avoided at all costs.

The two most common probate myths are that property is tied up and inaccessible for months, if not years, in probate and that the probate process is very expensive. Like all myths, there is a degree of truth to each. The truth of each will vary significantly from state to state as well. Most state probate systems are part of the state trial courts. However, probate courts and probate laws generally recognize the difficult circumstances of families passing through the probate process, and generally allow for the prompt appointment of an executor or administrator and provide access to funds as needed for the support of the family.

The costs also vary. Probate courts themselves have filing fees that may or may not be substantial. The greater cost, however, is the cost of legal and accounting fees that must be incurred in the process of administering an estate. Many probate courts, though certainly not all, are designed to allow the family to administer the estate without the assistance of counsel. Before assuming that the probate process is expensive and cumbersome, and thus important to avoid, an analysis of the probate process in the governing jurisdiction is necessary.

In reality, the most expensive and time-consuming aspect of estate administration is the preparation of the estate tax returns. This almost always requires professional assistance and costly appraisals. It also takes substantial time to prepare and, usually, months to have the return reviewed and approved by tax authorities. Without the need for tax returns, the process can proceed much more quickly and less expensively. None of the tools discussed above for avoiding probate will allow the decedent's estate to avoid preparing and filing tax returns if there is a taxable estate.[4] As the federal estate tax exemption increases to allow more estates to avoid tax-reporting requirements, the time and expense for smaller estates are diminished.

Another important issue to consider is whether there will be complicating factors or the likelihood of contests. In those cases, the probate process, with court oversight, may be desirable. However, the use of a revocable trust may reduce the risk of contests because, as a general rule, a legal heir who is excluded under a trust lacks standing to contest the terms of a trust but has an absolute right to contest a will. Unfortunately, the law is increasingly evolving to treat revocable living trusts like wills. The potential that the law will give any legal heir standing to contest the terms of a revocable trust does exist.

Another benefit of revocable trusts in some states is the ability to disinherit a spouse. Historically, a wife was entitled to an interest in her husband's estate, known as dower rights. In times when estates were entailed to the eldest sons and women could not own property, this promise of lifelong

---

[4] All assets owned by a revocable trust, held jointly or subject to a beneficiary designation, are still subject to estate tax, even if they are not subject to probate. See IRC §2038 and 2036 regarding taxation of revocable trusts and taxation of trusts where the grantor retains an income interest for life. A federal estate tax return is required for all estates that exceed the available exemption amounts, which are discussed in more detail later in the book. State estate tax rules and reporting requirements vary.

Introduction

protection for women was necessary. As women acquired the right to own property, husbands also were entitled to an interest in their wife's property at death, known as a curtsey. Over time in the United States, these dower and curtsey rights morphed into statutory rights of one spouse to take a share of the estate of a deceased spouse. Known traditionally as the "widow's share," they are now more commonly referred to by the more correct term of the "spousal elective share." The scope of the right varies by state, but typically they allow either spouse to elect to take an income interest in a fraction (typically one-half or one-third) of the estate of the deceased spouse. This effectively prevents one spouse from disinheriting another.

The right under the spousal elective share statutes initially applied only to the probate estate (i.e., assets that passed pursuant to a will). These statutes, in their traditional forms, would not apply to assets that pass under a revocable trust. This option allows a grantor to pass property to other beneficiaries without the risk of the spouse making a claim for the spousal elective share. This can be a valuable planning opportunity in lieu of a prenuptial agreement, or for spouses where divorce is pending. Unfortunately, some states, whether by statute or judicial fiat, have extended the spousal elective share rights to include an augmented probate estate, including assets held jointly, passing by beneficiary designation, and assets held in a revocable trust. In those states, the revocable trust is no longer viable as a means of disinheriting a spouse. A prenuptial agreement remains the most effective option where disinheritance is contemplated from the start, though it certainly is not guaranteed to work in all cases. For situations where spouses are separated but not yet divorced, these augmented estate laws will not allow for the disinheritance of the spouse.

The Impact of the Uniform Trust Code

American trust law evolved out of the Anglo-Saxon law of trusts, which most scholars trace to the time of the Crusades. In the feudal system, real property could not be held in abeyance. If the owner died and there was no immediate taker, the property escheated to the overlord. Knights traveling to the Holy Land to fight and likely die for the cause left their estates in the hands of trusted administrators (i.e., a trustee) to manage them until they returned or, if they were never to return, until their children were old enough to inherit. The law developed over the centuries with surprisingly little change and generally applied to all trusts without distinction. Unfortunately, over the last half a century, as the revocable living trust came into prominence as a will substitute, courts and some legislatures across the country developed a patchwork of decisions and laws treating revocable trusts more like wills and enhancing the rights of beneficiaries under revocable trusts.[5]

The "Restatement of the Law, Third, Trusts," published by the American Law Institute, is the cornerstone legal treatise that summarizes the historic and current case law regarding trusts throughout the country. In the absence of any direct local law on point with respect to trusts, courts typically would look to the Restatement (either the third edition or its predecessors) and adopt the rule set forth there, or some reasoned modification of the rule. Where the laws in several states diverge, the Restatement reflects both the majority rule and the minority rule. The third edition, which was started in the late 1980s and published in stages throughout the 1990s, reflects a distinct trend in the law toward enhancing the rights of beneficiaries. The National Conference of Commissioners of Uniform State Laws originally adopted the Uniform Trust Code in 2000, with amendments in 2001, 2003, and 2005, in an effort to establish the first national codification of trust law in close connection with the modern trend as reflected in the "Restatement of the Law, Third, Trusts." The purpose of the National Conference of Commissioners of Uniform State Laws is to establish laws that can be adopted in each state that will allow for uniformity in the law, rather than a patchwork of separate laws applied in each state. The "Prefatory Note" to the Uniform Trust Code explains the need for and purpose of the Code as follows:

> The primary stimulus to the Commissioners' drafting of the Uniform Trust Code is the greater use of trusts in recent years, both in family estate planning and in commercial transactions, both in the United States and internationally. This greater use of the trust, and consequent rise in the number of day-to-day questions involving trusts, has led to a recognition that the trust law

---

[5] See, for example, the Uniform Trust Code, Article 6.

Introduction 15

in many states is thin. It has also led to a recognition that the existing Uniform Acts relating to trusts, while numerous, are fragmentary. The Uniform Trust Code will provide states with precise, comprehensive, and easily accessible guidance on trust law questions. On issues on which states diverge or on which the law is unclear or unknown, the Code will for the first time provide a uniform rule. The Code also contains a number of innovative provisions.

The Uniform Trust Code's statement of purpose presents a compelling case for the need for uniform laws relating to trusts. However, the risk is in the final two sentences. States do have different rules, and the adoption of the Uniform Trust Code may dramatically change the rules that traditionally applied to trusts in each state. The introduction of "innovative provisions" also runs the risk of changing what otherwise would be well-settled law. The Uniform Trust Code has now been adopted in twenty-one states and has been introduced for acceptance in four more states. The Uniform Trust Code acknowledges that it establishes default rules that will apply only where the trust instrument is silent or inadequate to address a particular issue. (See Uniform Trust Code §105.)[6]

In this changing environment of trust law, it is essential that the terms of each trust document be considered carefully. Trusts now should be broader and more extensive, not simplified. For some time, academics and some practitioners have urged the simplification of trusts and other legal documents to make them easier for laypeople to understand and use. While it is important to do so, simplicity should never be adopted at the expense of specificity and legal accuracy. The key for a draftsman is to balance the need for understandable documents that are legally sufficient to meet all of the grantor's objectives, both the obvious overarching goals such as the identify of beneficiaries and the manner of distributions, as well as the more esoteric goals of administrative requirements. Reliance on the laws to accomplish desired goals of this later category is risky because that law is

---

[6] There are some rules in the Uniform Trust Code that cannot be overridden by the trust instrument, including the ability of a court to modify or terminate the trust, the rules relating to spendthrift provisions, and the obligation to notify certain beneficiaries regarding the trust.

likely to change over time and may be inconsistent with the intent of the grantor.

About This Book

This book is designed to illustrate the clauses ordinarily used in a revocable trust designed as a will substitute. The book is designed for those who are not trained in the law to understand the basic precepts of trust law and to understand how and why particular clauses are used, as well as for attorneys who are looking to understand the basic property and tax laws relating to trusts. Legal references to statutory provisions and important cases are set out in the text and in footnotes as a resource for those who are trained in the law and using this book as an aide to their practice.

The sample trust agreement is written in the first person. Many practitioners still prefer to write trust instruments in the third person, referring to "the Grantor intends" or "the Grantor's right" rather than "I intend" or "my right." There is nothing wrong with using the third person. Indeed, use of the first person in a trust instrument, as in contracts, was virtually unheard of even as late as the middle part of the last century, and many form books still use the third-person format. However, there has been an increasing trend in the law generally to use less formalistic language where possible. Although not all trends toward simplification are appropriate, the use of the first person can make a substantial and technical document less intimidating.[7] If the use of the third person is preferable, the sample trust language can easily be modified to do so. The sample trust also assumes for simplicity that the grantor is of the masculine gender—that he is married and has children. This gives the broadest range of clauses for discussion purposes. Obviously, if the grantor is not married or has no children, significant changes would need to be made to the sample document. Some alternative clauses are set forth in Appendix B. Typically, if the grantor is married, his spouse also would have a revocable trust with similar terms.[8]

---

[7] The use of the terms "the Grantor" and "the Trustee" was a progressive move toward clarification in an effort to move from the earlier formalistic references to the "party of the first part" and "the party of the second part."

[8] There has been a recent trend toward establishing joint trusts so that a couple can have a single trust for all of their assets and still obtain all of the tax benefits discussed in the

Introduction

This book is intended to provide a general overview of revocable trusts in the United States, and it does not address the law of any specific state. The text relies heavily on the Uniform Trust Code and the "Restatement of the Law, Third, Trusts" as they reflect the current trends in trust law. Trust law is governed by state law, and every state has variations on the general rules. Transfer tax rules are governed by separate state and federal laws. This book should not be viewed as the last word on the law as it relates to revocable living trusts, but merely as a starting point for general understanding. Before adopting a revocable trust as part of an estate plan, it is important to consult competent legal counsel in the jurisdiction where the trust will be established who is familiar with the trust law of his or her state. Those who suggest that one prefabricated form is valid and effective in all states are doing a disservice to the grantors, trustees, and beneficiaries who will be bound by the terms of such an instrument. While virtually any writing that names a trustee, identifies a beneficiary, and gives the barest of instructions for distribution of property will constitute a legally valid trust, it cannot fully express the goals and intent of the grantor without significant customization. The laws and courts of the governing jurisdiction will fill in the gaps that are not adequately addressed by the instrument. The need to resort to court interpretation will defeat the primary objective of establishing the trust in the first place. Indeed, the law may impose a result far different from what the grantor intended. Customization of the general clauses presented will be necessary in most cases.

A Word about Format

A revocable living trust is hardly a great work of literature. However, there should be a logical flow to the document. The beginnings of the trust instrument should set forth the nature of the instrument and any necessary definitions. The first substantive part should deal with administration

---

introduction to Article V. The use of joint trusts has been popular in community property states for some time, but there has been a movement toward using them in other states. The assumption is that a joint trust (i.e., one where both spouses are co-grantors of a trust that holds all of their property) will be cheaper to establish then two trusts, and will be simpler to administer. Neither of these assumptions is necessarily true. Also, there is some risk that the tax benefits will not be as effective under a joint trust as they are with separate trusts. A thorough discussion of the topic of joint trusts is beyond the scope of this book, but there are several interesting articles and private letter rulings issued by the Internal Revenue Service on this topic that are worth reviewing before adopting a joint trust. See PLR 200101021 and PLR 200210051.

during the life of the grantor, followed by the administration immediately following death, tantamount to the estate administration period. The following section should deal with administration for the benefit of the spouse and family (if there is a surviving spouse), followed by administration for the benefit of descendants after the death of both spouses. The final sections should deal with the appointment, powers, and administrative responsibilities of the trustee. Although other form documents may alter this format in some manner, this is the most logical flow, and it is the easiest to follow.

Before beginning the line-by-line analysis of each clause, it may be wise to set forth some of the basic terms used in talking about trusts.

- **Grantor:** The individual who creates the trust. The grantor may be called by many other names, including most commonly the settlor or the donor, and in some cases the trustor.

- **Corpus:** The property held in trust. This also is referred to by many other names, including principal, "*res*," or the "trust estate."

- **Trustee:** The individual or entity who holds legal title to the trust corpus. The trustee is generically referred to as a "fiduciary," which means the trustee holds legal title, but not beneficial title, and his or her ownership rights and responsibilities are limited by the terms of the instrument that created the trust and any applicable laws. The trustee has a variety of fiduciary duties with respect to protecting and preserving the property for the benefit of someone else (i.e., the beneficiaries).[9]

- **Beneficiary:** The individuals (or entities) for whom the trust corpus is held. They are sometime referred to as the beneficial owners of the property. For those who still prefer Latin, the term *cestui que* trust refers to the beneficiaries of the trust. The term

---

[9] The general duties of the trustee are not discussed in this book other than as relates to the specific clauses. For a general review of the duties of trustees, a review of the "Restatement of the Law, Third, Trusts," or other legal treatises on the topic, such as Charles E. Rounds Jr.'s *Loring Trustee's Handbook*, 2004 edition (Aspen Publishing), are instructive.

appears regularly in older cases, and occasionally in a few modern ones.

- **Trust agreement or trust declaration:** The written instrument that controls the terms of the trust.[10] If the grantor and the sole trustee are the same person, the instrument is referred to as a declaration of trust (since an individual cannot make an agreement, *per se*, with himself or herself). Where the grantor and the trustee are different, the instrument is referred to as a trust agreement. Even in a case where the grantor is one of the current trustees with a co-trustee, the instrument is nonetheless referred to as an agreement.

---

[10] Oral trusts are valid in most states, except where they would violate the Statute of Frauds. See, for example, Section 407 of the Uniform Trust Code, which requires clear and convincing evidence to prove the creation of an oral trust. Constructive and resulting trusts also may be created in the absence of any written instrument. However, these are equitable remedies rather then legal entities. Any intent to create a trust should be reduced to writing.

Line-by-Line Analysis

The Prefatory Sections

JOHN J. DOE REVOCABLE TRUST

This Trust Agreement is made on _____, 200__, by and between John J. Doe, (also known as Jack Doe) now residing in Anytown, Anystate, as Grantor, and John J. Doe and Mary M. Doe, now residing in Anytown, Anystate, as Trustees.

The opening clause of the trust agreement sets forth the key facts. First, it establishes the date of the agreement, which is important for identification purposes and to establish a timeline. It also identifies the grantor and trustees. This is typically done by use of a full name as well as any known aliases and an identification of the city and state of residence. A full address may be used, although this is apt to change over time and is not really necessary for identification purposes. Some older trust agreements may include a Social Security number as indisputable identification. While this is helpful proof of identification, it also is an unnecessary risk. The trust document often must be disclosed to a variety of individuals and entities. It is not recommended that the grantor's Social Security number be identified at any place in the trust instrument.

WHEREAS, I desire to transfer, assign and convey one dollar ($1.00) to the Trustees, together with any additional property acceptable to the Trustees that I or any other person may at any time transfer by beneficiary designation, assignment and delivery, or by gift, devise, bequest, appointment or otherwise, in order to establish a trust for the benefit of the beneficiaries named herein and for the purposes and subject to the terms and conditions set forth in this Agreement; and

WHEREAS, the Trustees acknowledge receipt of one dollar ($1.00) and agree to hold said property, together with any additions *thereto (hereinafter called the "trust estate"), in trust, for the purposes and subject to the terms and conditions set forth in this Agreement.*

NOW THEREFORE, I establish this trust, which shall be known as the "John J. Doe Revocable Trust," and which shall be administered as follows:

The "whereas clauses" describe the basic intent of the grantor to establish a trust and the willingness of the trustees to accept appointment and to be bound by the terms of the trust agreement. The use of "whereas clauses" is borrowed from contract law, where the identity of the parties and their intentions are typically set forth before establishing the terms of the contract. Trusts are similar to contracts in that they set up a binding agreement between the grantor and the trustee to administer the property subject to the trust for the benefit of the beneficiaries. However, trusts are governed by an entire body of law separate from contract law.

The use of "whereas clauses" is not necessary, but they are useful to make clear the intention to create a trust. Some form documents simply set forth the facts in these clauses in standard sentence format without the "whereas" reference. Giving the trust a name also is helpful for the ease of future reference. In their simplest form, as here, the "whereas clauses" should set forth the grantor's desire to establish a trust for the benefit of the beneficiaries and the trustee's willingness to accept the property in trust and to manage it pursuant to the terms of the trust agreement. Nothing more is needed in these clauses.

A trust cannot exist without a corpus (i.e., some property owned by the trustee as legal owner for the benefit of the beneficiaries pursuant to the terms of the governing instrument). This need for a corpus, sometimes referred to as the trust *res*, is one of the three fundamental tenants of trust law stemming from the earliest days of the common law. The requirement that there be a trustee and a beneficiary are the other two essential elements of a trust.[11] In its original context, this rule makes sense. If there was no

---

[11] Although the existence of a trustee is a prerequisite to the valid existence of a trust, a trust does not fail if there is no acting trustee. As long as there is some mechanism for the appointment of a trustee, the trust itself remains viable so long as there are beneficiaries and a corpus. Even in the absence of specific law allowing for the appointment of

property subject to the legal and beneficial ownership structure of a trust, there is no need of the trust. In the modern context of trust law where revocable trusts are used as a will substitute, many grantors create trusts with no intention of adding any property to the trust until some later date, potentially even only after death.

A trust without a corpus is a legal nullity. The rule that the trust is null and void for lack of a corpus would be catastrophic. Absent some protective statute, the future addition of property to the trust would not revive the trust, since it is treated as if the trust was never established. Thus, a will directing addition of the grantor's estate to a void trust would be an ineffective disposition, and intestacy would be the result. To prevent this dramatic and undesirable result, most revocable trusts assert that some nominal dollar amount is held in the trust from the start. This essentially is a legal fiction, but in acquiescence to the mandate of a corpus, some property must be subject to the trust from inception. The nominal amount used to establish the trust often is either $1, $5, or $10. Rarely would any larger amount be used, since having significant value in the trust would trigger fiduciary duties that may not be intended, such as a duty to prepare accountings.

If the grantor will, in fact, add assets to the trust immediately upon execution, it is possible, though not necessary, to set forth the actual assets that will be added to the trust rather than the nominal dollar amount. The trust agreement typically is given to a variety of people, including professional advisors, banks, beneficiaries, and the like. For privacy purposes, it may not be appropriate to have the assets of the trust listed within the trust documents. Since the reference to a nominal amount is sufficient to create the trust, and it is not necessary to amend the trust to reflect the addition of other assets, the nominal reference to a dollar amount typically is the preferred option.

---

trustees, courts of equity typically have the ability to appoint a trustee—hence the rule that no trust will fail merely because there is no acting trustee. See the "Restatement of the Law, Third, Trusts," Volume 1 for a detailed discussion of the fundamental elements of a trust.

Article I

[handwritten: VERY IMPORTANT]

Defining special terms used in the trust agreement is essential. Not all terms require a definition, but phrases that could be interpreted in multiple ways or that are intended to have a unique meaning should be defined to avoid confusion in interpreting the document. Some terms are set out in a separate definition section, as here in this "Definition of Terms" clause.[12] Other important terms are defined with parenthetical references throughout the document. Typically, those terms that require context to aid their meaning use the parenthetical definition, such as the definition of "trust estate" as used in the preface of the agreement in the preceding section.

Article I.   *Definition of Terms.*

As used in this Agreement, the following terms shall have the following meanings, unless otherwise expressly provided:

(A) ***Identification of Spouse.*** *I am married to Mary M. Doe. Any reference to "my wife" or "my spouse" shall be a reference only to Mary M. Doe and shall not include any person to whom I was or may be married at any other time. If my marriage to Mary M. Doe is legally terminated by divorce, annulment, legal separation or otherwise, then for all purposes under this Agreement (including her appointment as a Trustee) Mary M. Doe (as well as any relative of hers who is not also a descendant of mine) shall be deemed to have died on the date of such termination.*

(B) ***Identification of Children.*** *At present, my only children are Donald D. Doe and Debra D. Doe.*

(C) ***Definition of Children and Descendant.*** *The terms "child," "children," "descendant" and "descendants,"*

---

[12] The "Definition of Terms" clause does not need to appear at the beginning of the trust agreement. Indeed, in many cases, where a definitions clause is used, it often appears as a separate appendix or at the end of the document. Placing the definitions at the beginning can be distracting, and it may interrupt the flow of the document. However, because the definitions will be important to a proper understanding of the rest of the instrument, they are set forth here at the beginning.

Line-by-Line Analysis 25

> *or any similar term, with respect to any person shall include such person's present biological children and descendants, as well as any children or other descendants born after the date of this Agreement. In addition, such term shall include any child or descendant legally adopted by such person, before or after the date of this Agreement; provided such child or descendant was adopted prior to attaining age eighteen (18).*

Although the identification of family members may not seem like a definition, it is important to set forth the names of the grantor's spouse and children, whether or not they are beneficiaries under the trust agreement. Because revocable living trusts are often used as a substitute for a will, many courts and some legislatures have imposed rules of interpretation on trusts that ordinarily apply to wills. For example, under the common law, a will was revoked when the testator is divorced, remarried, or has another child. This remains the law in some states. Some jurisdictions have softened this rule to provide merely that the divorced spouse is cut out, but the balance of the will remains effective and by allowing after-born children to share equally with pre-born children. The testator always has the right to override these provisions for interpretation by the terms of the instrument. If, as in some jurisdictions, these will-based rules apply to trust interpretation, it is necessary to make provisions in the event of divorce, remarriage, and after-born children.

The definition of "spouse" identifies the current spouse and makes clear that any reference to the term "wife" or "spouse" will not include any past or future spouse. It also provides that if the grantor and his wife are divorced, she will be deemed to have predeceased the grantor. Although this seems unduly harsh, the reason for such language is to make clear that any role the spouse had, whether as a trustee or a beneficiary, is deemed to be moot, as it would be if she had, in fact, died before the grantor. It is possible to use less harsh terms, but none has proven quite as effective for accomplishing the complete exclusion of a divorced spouse. The date on which the interest of a divorcing spouse would terminate may be open to debate. Although it may seem preferable to terminate the spouse's interest upon filing for divorce, that would disinherit the spouse in the event of reconciliation before the divorce is final. Thus, it is best to limit termination of the spouse's right until the marriage is lawfully terminated. Assuming the grantor is capable, the trust should be modified immediately if divorce is pending or has been filed.

Relatives of the divorced spouse also are excluded. If a sibling of the spouse would receive a cash bequest or was named as a fiduciary, that sibling also would be cut out entirely by this clause. Before arbitrarily including this clause, it is important to consider whether it makes sense to exclude the spouse and her family members. If the spouse's sister is named as guardian and trustee for minor children, this clause would undermine that plan in the event of divorce. That may be appropriate, but it should not be assumed. Since the trust is revocable and can be changed, this merely helps protect the grantor who fails to make changes after a divorce, either through inadvertence or incapacity.

In defining children and descendants, whether they are of the grantor or of other parties to the trust, it is important to identify whether adopted children are included, and to set forth any limitations. The law generally provides that adopted children are children of the adopting parent and are not children of their biological parents for purpose of inheritances. Children of the half-blood ordinarily are treated the same as children of the whole blood. Step-children, however, typically are expressly excluded from inheritance unless they are adopted by the step-parent. To provide for a step-child, the step-child would need to be expressly identified as a beneficiary. Relying on the law, which may change, which may be different if the grantor moves to another state, or which simply is not consistent with the grantor's intent, is not a reasonable option with respect to identifying who will be permitted beneficiaries based on relationship.

Limiting the scope of adopted children to those adopted prior to age eighteen is an effort to prevent any attempt to acquire an inheritance right through adult adoption. As indicated, any adopted child is a legal child of the adopting parent without limitation on the age of the adoptee. By precluding adult adoptees, the grantor can prevent an improper effort to create an heir.[13] Some grantors may go further and exclude any child

---

[13] For a period of time, same-gender couples who were prohibited from marrying attempted to create legally recognized relationships for inheritance purposes through adult adoptions. This effort appears to have been unsuccessful in light of the sexual relationship between an adoptive "child" and "parent."

adopted over the age of six or twelve on the theory that only a child raised with the family should be a beneficiary. While there may be some merit in this approach, it often will have the effect of excluding step-children who are adopted, and it may also exclude some legitimate adoptions that experienced delay for one reason or another. In any event, the age limitation, or the lack of an age limitation, should be carefully considered and not adopted arbitrarily.

Where a legal heir,[14] such as a spouse or child, will be expressly excluded as a beneficiary, it is essential to set forth that exclusion in clear and unambiguous terms. For example, the following phrase is often employed:

> *I intentionally make no provisions under this agreement for my son, Donald D. Doe, for reasons that are known to my family. For all purposes under this Agreement, my son, Donald D. Doe, and all of his descendants shall be deemed to have predeceased me.*

This language makes the exclusion clear. If the reasons for the exclusion are benign, such as because one child is wealthy and the other has greater need of the inheritance, a phrase such as "not out of lack of love or affection, but for reasons that are known to my family" may be used. Note, however, that the reason for the exclusion is not set forth. Although it may feel right to set out the reasons for excluding a child, doing so can create problems of interpretation in the future. If, for example, a child is excluded because he is a drug addict and is completely disengaged from the family, what happens if the child stops using drugs? Will the child then get his inheritance? If the language excludes the grantor's son "because he is a drug addict," there will be a question of interpretation as to whether he should inherit if he stops using drugs, even temporarily. If that is the case, it should be spelled out expressly in the trust agreement and not left to interpretation.

(D) Definition of Education. The term "education," as used herein, shall include education at any level, including,

---

[14] The term "legal heir" refers to any individual who would inherit under the laws of intestacy if the testator died without a will. These laws vary by state, but typically the spouse and children are the first takers. If there is neither a spouse nor children, then parents, siblings, and the descendants of siblings, in varying degrees, are usually the next takers.

> but not limited to, preschool, elementary school, intermediate school, secondary school, college, graduate, post-graduate and professional training of any kind. It shall include, but is not necessarily limited to, the costs of tuition, fees imposed by any educational institution, books, supplies and the like. I intend that, under ordinary circumstances, the Trustees will interpret the term education liberally.

A surprising amount of controversy has arisen over the years regarding what is meant by the term "education." The definition provided here is very broad and should cover most traditional forms of education. It is important to consider the grantor's intentions, whether it may be appropriate to restrict the term by limiting it to specific forms of education, such as only "post-secondary" schools. Specificity in the definition provides clarity of purpose and gives guidance to the trustee of the grantor's intention. It also protects the trustee from claims by a beneficiary.

Education is not the only term that may benefit from a specific definition. A direction to make distributions for the "health" of a beneficiary also can be ambiguous. For example, it is not clear whether this would permit distribution for non-traditional medical procedures or the payment of medical insurance premiums. It would be nearly impossible to provide a complete list of all possible health-related matters for which distributions can be made. It may be sufficient to simply set forth a general expression as to whether the term "health" should be construed liberally and, perhaps, to set out a list of examples of health-related expenditures that would be appropriate.

As with defining health, the definition of "support" also may be too difficult to set into a simple paragraph. There is a relatively well-defined body of law governing what constitutes support. Thus, it makes sense to not provide a special definition of support unless there is a specific intent to place limitations on the term.

> **(E) Definition of Per Stirpes.** Notwithstanding the provision of any state's law to the contrary, whenever the Trustees are directed to distribute property to an individual's descendants or descendants "per stirpes," the

Line-by-Line Analysis   29

> *property shall be divided into shares beginning with the first generation below such individual, whether or not there are members of such generation living at the time of distribution. Subdivision of shares for successive generations shall be made in the same manner.*

Per stirpes is one of those classic Latin legal phrases that has survived because it is so useful. It represents a concept, in two words, that otherwise would require several sentences to explain. In short, *per stirpes* is a shorthand method of describing how assets will pass among a person's descendants, including how property will be divided if one or more descendants is deceased at the time of distribution. The problem, unfortunately, is that states do not have a uniform definition of *per stirpes* in their case law and statutes. Thus, it is necessary to provide a definition of the grantor's intended meaning, which will apply regardless of the interpretation state law would impose.

The following example demonstrates the different interpretations of the term. Assume G has three children, C1, C2, and C3. C1 has three children, GC1, GC2, and GC3. C2 has two children, GC4 and GC5. C3 has no children. If G dies survived by all three of his children and leaves $300,000 to his "descendants, *per stirpes*," the property would be divided equally ($100,000) among all three children and the grandchildren would receive nothing. If C1 predeceased G, his $100,000 would be divided equally among GC1, GC2, and GC3, but the other grandchildren would receive nothing. If C3 predeceased G, his $100,000 share would be distributed among C1 and C2, because C3 has no descendants.

For the most part, up to this point, all jurisdictions have the same definition of *per stirpes* and the results described would proceed under virtually all common law and statutory definitions, as well as under the definition used here. The distinction in definitions arises in a situation where all three of G's children predecease G. Under some jurisdictions, as well as the definition set forth here, the property would be divided at the first generation (i.e., the children), regardless of whether there are any members of that generation living. This is referred to as "setting the stocks." Under this definition, the $300,000 bequest would be divided with C3's share being divided between the shares determined with respect to C1 and C2.

C1's three children would share $150,000 ($50,000 each), and C2's two children would share $150,000 ($75,000 each).

Other jurisdictions set the stock in the first generation with living members. Since all of the children are deceased, the property would not be divided among the three children. Rather, in those jurisdictions, the stocks would be set at the grandchildren's generation, where there are five members, not three. Each grandchild would thus share one-fifth of the $300,000 ($60,000).

In the majority of cases, the definition of *per stirpes* may have little or no impact on the disposition of property, because children ordinarily survive their parent. However, where an entire generation is deceased, the definition can have significant economic impact on the beneficiaries. It should be noted that the statutory or common law definitions of *per stirpes* can always be overridden by the terms of the document. Thus, if state law would impose one result, but the grantor prefers a different result, he need only insert the definition of choice into the trust agreement. Even if the applicable state law is consistent with the grantor's intent, a definition is advisable in the event the jurisdiction of the trust changes and to avoid any ambiguity as to intention.

> **(F) Definition of Trustee.** *Any reference to "the Trustee" or "the Trustees" shall encompass all Trustees then acting, including any Independent Trustee. The use of the singular shall be deemed to include the plural if there is more than one Trustee then acting, and the use of the plural shall include the singular if there is only one Trustee then acting. Any use of personal pronouns indicative of gender shall be deemed to include the masculine, feminine and neuter genders, as applicable. The Trustees also are sometimes referred to herein as "fiduciaries." Unless otherwise provided, any Trustee acting under this Agreement may exercise all of the rights, powers and discretions and shall be entitled to all of the privileges and immunities granted to the named Trustee.*

More than a definition, this clause is a savings provision to clarify that the use of the singular or plural or personal pronouns are demonstrative only, and do not require the existence of a certain number of or a particular gender for the trustees. Undoubtedly, this language is overkill, much like a warning on a box of knives that the contents are sharp. Nonetheless, these issues have been a source of litigation, and the wise lawyer includes this type of savings clause in virtually all contracts and trust agreements. Of only slightly more merit is the final sentence, which affirms that all trustees are created equally and have the same rights and responsibilities as the initially named trustee. The first sentence does, however, make clear that any time an action is required by "the Trustee(s)," all trustees, including an independent trustee, must act, as distinguished from the references to the "Independent Trustees," where only a trustee meeting specific qualifications, as set forth in the next clause, may act.

Ordinarily, unless the trust agreement expressly provides otherwise, where there are multiple trustees, all of the trustees must act unanimously. This can create deadlock, especially where there are three or more trustees. It is permissible to incorporate a provision that trustees may act by majority rule rather than unanimously. If that option is desired, it must be expressly included. Language similar to the following (typically included in either Article X or Article XII) is used:

> **Majority Rules.** *Any discretionary decision may be made by a majority of the Trustees then acting and unanimity is not required. If any Trustee does not consent to a decision made by the majority of Trustees, the non-consenting Trustee shall not be liable for any action or inaction resulting from such decision.*

It is important to protect the non-consenting trustee from liability in cases where majority rule is allowed. Where the spouse is one of the trustees, it may be desirable to require that the majority cannot act without the consent of the spouse. Additional language such as this, added to the end of the first sentence, may be used to accomplish that restriction: "provided, however, that if my spouse is acting as a Trustee, no decision of a majority of the Trustees shall control unless my spouse consents to such decision."

(G) Definition of Independent Trustee. For the purposes of this Agreement, a Trustee is an "Independent Trustee" only if such Trustee meets the following criteria: (i) is not a beneficiary currently eligible to receive the income or principal of the trust; (ii) is not a beneficiary who would be eligible to receive the income or principal of the trust if the trust were to terminate at the time the discretionary decision is made; (iii) is not the spouse, sibling, ancestor or descendant of a beneficiary described in subpart (i) or (ii); and (iv) in the case of any Trustee who is appointed by one or more of the beneficiaries described in subpart (i) or (ii), would not be a related or subordinate party with respect to any beneficiary who exercised the power to appoint such Trustee.

(H) Definition of Related or Subordinate Party. The term "related or subordinate party" used with respect to any person shall have the same meaning as provided in section 672(c) of the Code, as if such person were the Grantor of the trust.

Unlike the prior clause, the definition of the "independent trustee" is critically important. Throughout the trust agreement, there are a variety of trustee powers that can only be exercised by an independent trustee. There are significant tax and creditor problems that may arise when a beneficiary acts as trustee of his or her own trust. Thus, to avoid these problems, it is important to preclude the beneficiary-trustee from exercising certain powers that would create those problems. Simplistically, the independent trustee could be defined as any trustee who is not a current or future beneficiary of the trust. That would protect against most tax and creditor protection concerns. However, subparts (iii) and (iv) above are included out of an abundance of caution. To prevent a person closely related to the beneficiary from making the decision gives the trustee a greater degree of independence. Also, by precluding the beneficiary from appointing a

Line-by-Line Analysis

subservient person to make the decision also helps to prevents abuse of these powers.[15]

Use or incorporation of external legal provisions.

> **(I) Definition of Code.** The term "Code" whenever used herein shall mean the Internal Revenue Code of 1986, as amended, or any corresponding provision of any subsequent Federal tax law, together with any regulations, proposed regulations or temporary regulations relating thereto.

Defining the code may be yet another superfluous act. Every few decades, Congress seems to enact a complete overhaul of the tax laws. Were trusts are designed to last for many years, the tax law in effect when the trust was written will undoubtedly change over time while the trust is in existence. To the extent tax code provisions would be relevant to the interpretation of the trust agreement, the rules of interpretation would require the trustee, the beneficiaries, and the courts to look to the law in effect at the time the trust was established. Thus, defining which tax code applies probably has little legal significance. Nonetheless, it is worth including a definition to give future readers a quick reference to the applicable code and highlighting the fact that the code at issue may be different from the then-governing law.

Who determines incapacitation.

> **(J) Definition of Incapacity.** An individual shall be considered to be incapacitated if the individual (i) is under a legal disability, or (ii) is unable to give prompt and intelligent consideration to financial matters by reason of illness, mental or physical disability, or (3) has disappeared or is unaccountable absent. The determination as to whether an individual is incapacitated shall be made by the Trustees (other than such individual), or, if none, by the institution or individual designated to succeed such individual as Trustee, or, if none, by a majority of the beneficiaries then entitled to income of the trust. In making the determination, the Trustees may rely conclusively upon (i) the written opinion of either the individual's primary physician or any other two (2) board certified physicians (which certification

---

[15] A detailed discussion of the term "related or subordinate party" and the tax implications associated with the need for an independent trustee are set out in detail in the discussion of Article X, relating to the removal of trustees.

> *is in the area of medicine most proximately related to the cause of the disability) stating that the individual is under a legal disability or is unable to give prompt and intelligent consideration to financial matters by reason of illness or mental or physical disability; (ii) the receipt of credible evidence that such individual has disappeared or is unaccountably absent; or (iii) the written order of any court. To enable the Trustees to obtain such opinions, I and all Trustees accepting their appointment as Trustee hereby waive any patient-doctor privilege or other privacy claims relating to information in the possession of any physician regarding such individual's mental or physical condition.*

It is common to provide that a trustee will automatically cease to act if the trustee becomes incapacitated, in order to allow the successor trustee to assume responsibility for the trust. In addition, there may be other dispositive trust provisions that are contingent on a determination of whether an individual is incapacitated. The basis upon which a determination of capacity will be made needs to be clearly articulated to avoid potential disputes in the future. Legal definitions of incapacity may be far too stringent to satisfy the need to remove a trustee who cannot adequately manage a trust. Incapacity, for purposes of a trust, does not necessarily incorporate the full universe of disabilities. Physical incapacity would not necessarily preclude one from effectively serving as trustee. Some mental or emotional infirmity also would not necessarily preclude service as a trustee. Realistically, the only incapacity that matters is the inability to handle financial matters in a prudent manner. This incapacity most often is a result of a physical or mental disability, but it can also arise as a result of absence, such as a member of the military called to service. A trustee who is under a "legal disability" would be one where the law prescribes a finding of a lack of ability to engage in certain activities. For example, the mere fact of being a minor would be a legal disability, and the minor could not serve as trustee.

Once a definition of incapacity is established, it is necessary to set forth who can make the determination that a lack of capacity exists. Logically, the other acting trustees, or a successor trustee, would make that determination. It would be possible, in the alternative, to allow the determination to be

Line-by-Line Analysis   35

made by the beneficiaries (or a majority of the beneficiaries) or by a court. Using a combination of these options would likely provide the greatest degree of protection from any one person having too much power and the risk that it may be abused. For example, the clause might use the conjunctive of the trustees "and" a majority of the eligible income beneficiaries. The question really turns upon whether the grantor prefers to vest this level of authority in the trustees without the approval of the beneficiaries. The clause as drafted shows a preference for the power of the trustee. Where the preference is to place greater power in the hands of the beneficiaries, an alternate clause should be considered.

Regardless of who has the power to make a determination that an individual is incapacitated, allowing the decision to be made in the absence of credible medical evidence would not be prudent. Typically, it is reasonable to rely on the determination of a person's primary care physician. It is to be expected that a primary physician who has seen a person over the course of several years would be qualified to make a determination of capacity. This assumes, of course, that a primary physician has a longstanding relationship with the patient. In reality, a physician may be named as a primary physician even before the first visit. If the decision-maker is not relying on a primary physician with personal knowledge of the presumed-incapable person, another physician or two could make the determination. This clause requires an opinion of two physicians to mitigate the risk of an invalid diagnosis, but that is not mandatory. Further, the clause requires that physicians be board-certified in the area of medicine most relevant to the cause of the alleged incapacity. It would not do to have an opinion of a podiatrist finding lack of capacity due to dementia.

As a fail-safe provision, it is wise to give ultimate authority to a court to determine incapacity if all other options fail. Courts are regularly called upon to evaluate the capacity of an individual to manage his or her financial affairs in the contexts of guardianship and conservator matters. There are well-developed bodies of law supporting this determination. Though the goal is always to avoid court when possible through careful drafting, the option of resorting to courts when necessary is a consistent theme through the sample trust agreement.

(K) Definition of Death Taxes. *The term "death taxes," as used herein, shall mean any estate, transfer, excise, succession, inheritance, legacy, and other similar taxes (including any generation-skipping transfer tax, unless otherwise expressly provided) imposed by the federal government, any state, municipality, foreign government or any other tax authority by reason of my death. It also shall include any interest and penalties properly imposed thereon.*

The phrase "death tax" has taken on a life of its own since the anti-tax politicians co-opted the term as a pejorative reference to the federal estate tax in their efforts to repeal the tax. However, estate-planning practitioners have long used the term "death taxes" as a short-hand description for a variety of taxes that are imposed on the transfer of property by reason of a person's death. These include estate taxes at both the state and federal levels, as well as a host of similar taxes such as an inheritance tax. The estate tax is a tax imposed on the estate of a decedent for the privilege of transferring wealth at death. An inheritance tax, by contrast, is imposed on the beneficiary of the property for the privilege of receiving wealth at the death of another. The generation-skipping transfer (GST) tax also is imposed at death, and it is an additional tax imposed on the privilege of transferring property to an individual who is more than one generation junior to the transferor.[16] The definition of death taxes is designed to encompass all of the possible taxes that are imposed on transfers at death. It should be as broad as possible. Where necessary, the broad term can be limited by express provisions elsewhere in the documents.

Article II

Article II. **Grantor Retained Rights.**

I reserve the right to amend or revoke this Agreement, and the estates and interests hereby created, in whole or in part. Any such revocation or amendment shall be in writing, signed and acknowledged by me, and delivered to each Trustee then acting. Notwithstanding the foregoing, the duties and obligations of the Trustees hereunder shall

---

[16] The estate tax and GST tax are discussed in substantial detail in the introduction to Article V.

not be increased without their written consent. The rights under this Article are personal to me and may not be exercised by any person acting on my behalf in a fiduciary capacity.

This article sets forth the right of the grantor to alter or amend the terms of the trust agreement at any time. Many practitioners consider this standard boilerplate language, and they often bury it back in the body of the trust. Placement of the clause is far less important than the language used, since the right to change the trust is the fundamental aspect of the trust from both a practical and tax perspective. A trust that cannot be changed is no longer a will substitute, but rather a complete transfer of the trust estate to the trust beneficiaries. Traditionally, the law presumes that if a trust instrument is silent regarding the ability to amend or revoke the trust, it will be an irrevocable trust.

This clause indicates that the right to amend or revoke the trust is personal to the grantor and cannot be exercised by anyone else. It is important to consider carefully whether this final sentence is appropriate in each circumstance. The intent of this clause is that only the grantor can make changes to his trust document. If a conservator or guardian is appointed for the grantor in the event of incapacity, or if the grantor has appointed an agent under a durable power of attorney, those fiduciaries would not have the right to make changes to his trust agreement. As a theoretical matter, it makes sense to preclude anyone but the grantor from changing the trust instrument, because only the grantor knows unequivocally what he wants to happen with his assets at his death. However, as a practical matter, if there is a problem with the document and it is discovered after the grantor becomes incapacitated but before death, those changes cannot be made. Also, if circumstances or tax laws change, revisions could not be made.

On balance, however, it would be an extraordinary circumstance where a grantor would actually want to give someone else the unrestricted power to change the disposition of his estate. In that regard, a revocable trust is not different from a will, since a will also cannot be modified after the testator becomes incapacitated. Allowing an agent to make changes to a revocable trust should be done only after very careful consideration and consultation with counsel. If, under the worst case scenario, an error or problem is discovered and the grantor is unable to make changes, most states allow a petition to a court to reform the document if doing so would be consistent with the grantor's intention. For example, if there is a clause that would cause tax liability that was unintended, the trustee or the beneficiaries can petition the court to reform that clause by demonstrating that the grantor's purpose was to save taxes for his family and not to cause additional taxes. This option further reduces the need to allow someone other than the grantor to make changes to the document. Also, the risk that an agent can make a change to the document in favor of himself would constitute a general power of appointment and would result in adverse estate tax consequences for the holder of the power. Thus if this power is given to any person, it should be strictly circumscribed to avoid tax liability.[17]

Article III

This first substantive article sets forth the terms of the disposition of trust assets while the grantor is living. It is important to maximize the rights of the grantor as a *beneficiary* of the trust. Although the grantor is a trustee, his powers as trustee will be effective only so long as he is capable. Also, his rights as trustee may be circumscribed by his duty to future beneficiaries. Thus, broad rights as the primary beneficiary must be established for the grantor.

> **Article III.**   *Trust during My Lifetime.*
>
> *During my lifetime, the trust estate shall be administered as follows:*
>
> > **(A) Distributions.** *The Trustees shall pay to me or for my benefit so much or all of the net income and principal of the trust as I may request from time to time. If, in the opinion of the Trustees (other than me), or the named successor Trustee if there is no other Trustee then acting, I am incapacitated, the Trustees may distribute to or for the benefit of me or my spouse so much or all of the net income and principal of the trust as the Trustees consider advisable to provide adequately for the education, maintenance in health and reasonable comfort, and support in accustomed*

---

[17] See the discussion under Section A of Article 3 regarding the tax implications of powers of appointment.

> *manner of living of my spouse and me. The Trustees shall accumulate and add to principal at least annually any net income not so paid.*

The provisions regarding distribution should give the grantor unlimited access to the property while he is alive and competent. The grantor has the ability to withdraw all assets and to direct how the assets are distributed. Whether or not the grantor is the trustee or a co-trustee, this broad access language should be included. He also should be the sole beneficiary. If the grantor desires to make transfers to any other person while he is living and able, he can do so by withdrawing and gifting assets.

If the grantor becomes incapacitated, he will no longer be able to request distributions for himself. In that event, distributions should be authorized for the benefit of the grantor and his spouse. It is possible to include a provision that allows for distribution to the grantor's children. However, so long as a spouse is a beneficiary, typically it is not necessary to provide for distributions to children. If the children are minors, the trustee can make distributions for the benefit of the grantor's minor children without specifically naming the children as beneficiaries, because it is the grantor's obligation to support his minor children. Any distributions that are made to children from the trust, other than pursuant to a support obligation, would be gifts to the children and potentially are subject to gift taxes. Also, if the children are eligible beneficiaries while the grantor is alive, the trustee will have divided loyalties and will be obligated to consider the needs of the children in making distribution decisions.[18]

If the grantor and his spouse are co-trustees, or if the spouse will become a trustee in the event that the grantor is incapacitated, it is essential to limit the spouse's ability to take assets from the trust. If the spouse has unlimited access to her husband's trust assets, she is deemed to have a general power of appointment over the trust assets. When she dies, all of the assets in her husband's trust would be subject to tax in her estate. To avoid this problem, the clause provides that, if the grantor becomes incapacitated, distributions

---

[18] Note, however, that Section 603 of the Uniform Trust Code overrides this traditional rule and provides that the trustee of a revocable trust owes his exclusive duty to the grantor while the grantor is alive and capable.

can be made to both the grantor and his spouse, but only for their "health, education, and support in accustomed manner of living."

This is the first of many times this language appears in the sample trust agreement. Where the trustee is a beneficiary of a trust, and the beneficiary-trustee has the right to make unlimited distributions of trust assets to herself, the power is a general power of appointment. Under IRC §2041, any property subject to a general power of appointment is subject to estate tax at the death of the power-holder. This means property in the trust would be subject to tax at the death of the spouse if she predeceases the grantor.

If the power of the beneficiary-trustee to access the trust property is limited by an ascertainable standard, the power to invade or consume trust property is not a general power of appointment, and the trust property is not subject to tax at the death of the spouse. Internal Revenue Code Regulation §20.2041-1(c)(2) provides the types of restrictions that will constitute an ascertainable standard. The regulation provides that an ascertainable standard exists if it is "reasonably measurable in terms of his needs for health, education, or support (or any combination of them)." The regulation goes on to provide the following examples of powers that would be considered to be limited by the requisite standard: "support," "support in reasonable comfort," "maintenance in health and reasonable comfort," "support in his accustomed manner of living," "education, including college and professional education," "health," and "medical, dental, hospital, and nursing expenses and expenses of invalidism." Most standard trust forms adopt some combination of these standards to protect a beneficiary-trustee from estate tax liability. If a beneficiary will act as trustee, it is essential that language of this nature be included in the trust instrument to protect the trustee from unexpected tax liability. Other specific restriction, such as "for a wedding" or "to start a business" or "to purchase a home," while not expressly set forth in the regulations, are adequately specific to qualify as an ascertainable standard, because the trustee can be held to account to the beneficiaries for failing to meet such a standard. The regulations are clear that a standard simply for "comfort," "welfare," or "happiness" will not qualify as an ascertainable standard. Terms of this nature should be avoided.

This clause also provides that the trustee may accumulate income in the trust. This is important to make clear that the trustee is not obligated to distribute all of the income each year to the grantor.

> **(B)** *Limited Distributions to Agent for Gifts.*
> *Without limiting the generality of the foregoing, if, in the opinion of the Trustees (other than me), or the named successor Trustee, if there is no other Trustee then acting, I am incapacitated, the Independent Trustee is specifically authorized to distribute to my agent or to any person or entity identified by my agent acting under a durable power of attorney executed by me such amounts as my agent specifically requests, in order to begin or continue any gift-giving program established by me. The power to make distribution to my agent shall be limited in scope and manner to permit the agent to make gifts in the manner expressly set forth in the durable power of attorney executed by me in favor of such agent.*

There is significant debate among practitioners and academics as to whether a revocable living trust should grant a power to make gifts to an agent after the grantor becomes incapacitated. If the grantor intends to fully fund the revocable living trust with all of his assets before death in order to avoid probate and to provide management of his assets during incapacity, the gift authority may be necessary for several reasons. Elder law attorneys will argue that the power is needed to allow for the depletion of the grantor's estate in order to qualify for long-term care assistance. Estate tax planning attorneys will argue that the power is necessary to allow gifting in order to reduce the grantor's taxable estate to reduce estate tax liability. From a practical perspective, gifting may be necessary if the grantor was committed to a gifting program. If the grantor was assisting grandchildren with college tuition or paying premiums on a policy owned by an insurance trust, those gifts would need to stop at the incapacity of the grantor in the absence of a gifting power within the trust agreement.

The risk of including a gifting power is that the power may be treated as a general power of appointment over the trust assets. This would cause the entire trust estate to be included in the estate of the holder of the power. In an effort to balance the need for a gifting power against the risk of taxability to the holder of the power, this clause allows an agent named under a durable power of attorney executed by the grantor to request distributions in order to either start gifting or continue a gifting program previously initiated by the grantor. This power could not be exercised by a court-appointed guardian or conservator.

The agent's power is limited by the terms of the durable power of attorney in his favor. This means it is critical for the grantor to exercise a durable power of attorney at the same time as the trust agreement. The identity of the agent will inform how the gifting power should be limited. Gifts to the spouse are not taxable and may be unlimited. Gifts to descendants are taxable if they exceed a certain amount set forth in IRC §2503(b). Thus, the durable power of attorney should limit the amount of annual gifts to descendants to the amount permitted to pass tax-free annually. If the agent is also a permitted recipient of the gifts, this limitation is essential to avoid adverse tax liability for the agent.[19] Before incorporating a gifting power for an agent, it is important to weigh the risks against the benefits. This power should be given only if it is likely to be necessary.

> **(C) Termination.** *At my death, this trust shall terminate and any remaining property of the trust estate, together with any property added to the trust estate by reason of my death, shall be disposed of pursuant to Article IV of this Agreement.*

The termination clause merely provides that when the grantor dies, the living trust component will terminate and the remaining trust property, as well as any property that is added into the trust because the grantor has died, will be disposed of pursuant to the following article of the trust agreement. For example, assets may be directed into the trust under the grantor's will or by a beneficiary designation form for retirement assets or life insurance.

---

[19] The risk remains that the amount subject to the agent's gifting power will be treated as a general power of appointment at death, and will be taxable in the agent's estate if he predeceases the grantor. Also, each year that the gifting power is not exercised may be treated as a lapse of a general power of appointment that may be treated as a gift by the power-holder. See IRC §2514. So long as the amount is limited to the annual exclusion amount, the consequences of taxability is relatively minor.

Line-by-Line Analysis

Article IV

When the grantor of a revocable living trust dies, the trust is the functional equivalent of an estate. In some cases, the grantor who has not fully funded his trust will have a separate probate estate and an executor named to administer the estate. In cases where the trust is fully funded, there will be no separate probate estate and no executor. Many of the responsibilities that ordinarily fall to the executor would, in the later case, need to be handled by the trustee. The trustee would prepare returns and pay death taxes, and would be responsible for paying the grantor's debts and the cost of administration. The trust agreement must deal with both contingencies.

> **Article IV.** *Disposition upon Death of Grantor.*
>
> *Any property directed to be disposed of pursuant to this Article shall be disposed of as follows:*
>
> **(A)** *Payment of Expenses, Debts and Taxes.*
>
> **1.** *Payment to or for Executor.* The Trustees shall pay to or on behalf of the Executor of my estate or other personal representative ("the Executor"), out of the principal of the trust estate such amount or amounts as the Executor requests in writing for my funeral expenses, the expenses of administering my estate, any preresiduary gifts under my Will and any death taxes that are required by my Will to be paid as an administration expense. If an Executor is appointed to administer my estate, the Trustees may rely conclusively on the written certification of the Executor as to the amount or amounts to be paid pursuant to this section.
>
> **2.** *Direct Payment.* If no Executor is appointed to administer my estate, the Trustees shall pay, out of the trust estate as an administration expense, my funeral expenses, the expenses of administering my estate, and any death taxes, other than any generation-skipping

transfer tax, imposed upon or with respect to property that passes (i) under this Agreement, or (ii) from or under any retirement plan , trust or account (whether or not qualified under section 401, 403 408 or 408A of the Code) that passes outright to or in trust for the benefit of my spouse and/or my descendants at my death.

3. ***Proration, Apportionment and Recovery.*** *Any debts, death taxes or expenses that are directed to be paid out of the trust estate shall be paid without proration or apportionment against any beneficiary under this Agreement and without any statutory rights to recover any amounts so paid. All other death taxes not directed to be paid out of the trust estate as an administration expense pursuant to this section shall be prorated and apportioned in the manner provided by law with all applicable rights of recovery.*

The first three subsections of Section A set forth the instructions with respect to payment of taxes. While this is likely to be one of the more technical and most tedious provisions of the trust instrument, it is among the most important. The law in each state (and some federal rules) sets forth default provisions for the manner in which death taxes are to be paid, unless the testator instructs otherwise. As a general rule, these statutes tend to provide that tax liability will be allocated among the beneficiaries in proportion to the share of the estate that each receives. For example, if one child receives two-thirds of the estate and another child receives one-third of the estate, the child who receives two-thirds of the estate will pay two-thirds of the tax liability and the other child will pay one-third of the tax liability.

No discussion of the importance of drafting a proper tax clause would be complete without examples of horror stories that result from poor planning. An infamous story of the impact of the tax clause involves the life and death of a famous news personality. The testator left his entire estate to his spouse under his will and provided that the taxes on all property subject to tax in his estate would be borne by his residuary estate. In a holographic codicil, the testator left a valuable ranch to his secret mistress of thirty years, generating a substantial tax. Adding insult to injury, the Montana Supreme Court concluded that the tax clause in the will required the tax generated by the devise of the ranch to be paid out of the residue that otherwise passed to the wife.[20] It is unlikely the testator understood the impact of the decision with respect to the tax clause, as he probably had no legal advice with respect to the holographic codicil. It is not clear whether he would have chosen this result if he had known. However, it is essential that the grantor of a revocable trust understand the impact that his tax clause will have on the relative interests of the beneficiaries of his estate.

The grantor can override the statutory presumption and have all of the taxes paid off the top before the remaining trust estate is distributed in whatever proportions the grantor provides.[21] Many tax clauses (as was the case in *Kuralt*) are drafted so that taxes are all paid off the top, and then the remaining assets are distributed among the beneficiaries as provided in the instrument. This often is done as a default with little or no thought. As has been shown, this can be problematic where there are significant assets that pass outside the will or trust, such as by beneficiary designation or joint ownership, or where there is a pre-residuary bequest. In such cases, the tax liability may be greater than the value of the residue. Where the residuary and non-residuary beneficiaries are the same, this result is not particularly problematic. The problem arises when the beneficiaries are different and the non-residuary beneficiaries receive their inheritance tax-free while the residuary beneficiaries bear the full burden of the tax, potentially to the point of complete disinheritance.

It is possible, and in some cases desirable, to have certain beneficiaries bear the responsibility for the taxes generated from the bequest they receive. For example, if the grantor leaves valuable real estate to his brother, and the rest

---

[20] *Estate of Kuralt*, 2003 MT 92 (Mont. Sup. Ct. 2003). The Montana Supreme Court enumerated this case as *Kuralt, IV*, because there were several separate cases relating to this estate.

[21] It is essential that if the grantor has a will, it must contain a corresponding provision regarding the payment of taxes that is consistent with the terms of the trust. In some states, the statutory tax apportionment clause can only be overridden in a will. In such states, a will would be necessary even if the testator had no probatable assets because his revocable trust was fully funded prior to death.

of his estate to his children, the allocation of tax liability will have a significant impact on the relative inheritance of each. If the tax clause requires that *all* taxes be paid from the residue, the brother will receive his property free of tax and the children will bear all of the tax liability for both the real estate and the residue. If instead the tax clause requires complete apportionment, then each will be liable for a proportionate share of the tax. The proportion of the beneficiary's tax liability is calculated using the fraction of the beneficiary's share of the estate over the total estate multiplied by the total tax liability. Thus, if the real estate is worth $200,000 and the total estate is worth $1 million, the brother's share of the estate is one-fifth of the total estate. If the total tax due is $100,000, the brother's share of the tax liability would be $20,000 (or one-fifth of $100,000).[22]

The tax clause as drafted here is more circumscribed than full payment by the residue, but broader than strict apportionment. This clause directs that the residue will bear the taxes for only certain items. It provides instructions for the trustee under Subsection 1 in the event there is an executor and under Subsection 2 if there is no executor.

Under Subsection 1, if an executor is appointed to administer the decedent's estate, the trustee may use any of the trust property to pay for any of the debts of or claims against the grantor, any taxes that are due because of the grantor's death, and any expenses of administering his estate. The trustee is permitted to rely on instructions from the executor regarding amounts due, rather than doing his own analysis. In many cases, as a practical matter, the trustee and the executor should be the same person. The grantor's will should have a corresponding provision instructing the executor to seek payment from the trust if the probate estate is insufficient.

---

[22] Another significant example is where a bequest (or a portion of the residue) is payable directly to a grandchild. In that case, an estate tax is payable and a second tax, known as a generation-skipping transfer tax, also is payable. On a bequest of $100,000 to a grandchild, it is possible that about $70,000 of taxes will be due. It may not be appropriate for the other beneficiaries to pay this double tax. This clause, in the first sentence of Subsection 2, excludes the payment of GST tax from the trust. As a result, the tax will be borne by the beneficiary who receives the distribution. It is presumed that the grantor would not want the other residuary beneficiaries to bear the burden of such an extraordinarily high tax where they receive no benefit from the property passing to the grandchild. However, it is important to ascertain the grantor's intent before adopting such a provision. See the introduction to Article V for a discussion of the GST tax.

Because one of the primary purposes of using a revocable trust is to avoid probate of estate assets, in many cases an executor will not be appointed for the grantor's estate. In such cases, allowing reliance on the executor would be moot. For that reason, Subsection 2 of this clause gives the trustee the discretion to determine what expenses are due and payable because of the decedent's death, and to make those payments as if he was the executor of the estate. The clause as written in Subdivision (i) provides that any taxes generated from assets held by the trust will be borne by the trust. Taxes on trust property will not be apportioned among the beneficiaries as discussed above. It is possible to require that taxes on non-trust property be borne out of the trust residue as well. For example, as drafted, if there is a life insurance policy payable to one child, under the current clause, there would be no tax paid on that life insurance policy out of the residue. Rather, the beneficiary of the policy would pay any tax associated with that asset. If the grantor wanted the trust residue to pay the taxes rather than the beneficiary of the insurance policy, it should be set forth in this clause that any tax associated with that policy would be borne by the trust. Language such as the following could be used to accomplish this: "(ii) any life insurance policy on my life payable by reason of my death [to my son, Donald])." The parenthetical will limit the reference to only policies that are payable to a particular beneficiary. Without the parenthetical limitation, all taxes on all policies would be borne by the residue.

Subdivision (ii) of the sample clause provides that the trust residue also will pay the taxes generated by any retirement assets that are paid to either the grantor's spouse or his descendents. Without this clause, the beneficiary of the retirement account would be required to pay those taxes. Retirement accounts are generally created with tax-exempt funds and are subject to two layers of taxation when the participant dies. First, they are subject to the estate tax when the participant dies. Second, as the property is taken out of the retirement account by the beneficiary, it is also subject to income tax. This combined tax could be in the range of 70 percent. Therefore, if a beneficiary receives retirement assets and is required to pay the estate tax out of the retirement assets, he may have to pay the estate tax by taking money out of the retirement account. Withdrawal from the account to pay estate taxes would result in income tax liability. This could substantially eviscerate the retirement account, leaving very little or nothing for the beneficiary. Because of the income tax-free growth of retirement assets, it is usually preferable to preserve these assets when possible.

For this reason, it makes sense for the grantor to have the trust pay the estate taxes on the retirement assets so the beneficiary is not forced to pay an immediate income tax on the retirement assets. However, before adopting this provision, it is essential to consider the identity of the beneficiaries of the account and the trust. If the beneficiaries are the same, the payment of the retirement account liability from the trust has only a positive income tax advantage. If the identity is different, the trust beneficiaries will bear the liability for assets that do not pass to them. For example, if the beneficiary of the retirement account is a second spouse, and the beneficiaries of the trust are children of a prior marriage, it may not be fair to have the children paying the taxes on the asset that passes to their step-mother. Although generally paying the taxes on the retirement accounts out of the trust estate makes sense from a tax perspective, it may have an unanticipated adverse effect on the family estate plan. This impact should be considered before adopting a clause of this nature.

The payment of debts, taxes, and expenses from the trust estate are all directed to be paid "out of the trust estate as an administration expense." This language is designed to allow the payment of these items to qualify for an estate tax deduction. Local law on the deductibility of these items for probate accounting purposes may vary. However, by including this language, the payment of these items as an administration expense will allow the trustee or executor to take a deduction for the payment on the estate tax return.

Subsection 3 provides that if Subsection 2 directs that assets are to be paid out of the trust estate as an administration expense, it is paid from the residue. The trust beneficiaries will not bear a share of the taxes in proportion to their inheritance. The trustee will not prorate the shares or allocate liability proportionately, nor will the trustee seek recovery from the beneficiary for the payment of any tax. In the absence of this clause, all of those options may be available under state or federal tax law. This language is the express direction to opt out of the statutory proration scheme. With respect to any other tax that is not specifically directed to be paid from the trust estate (such as the tax on the insurance policy discussed above) this clause directs that the tax will be borne by the beneficiary in the manner provided by law (i.e., through apportionment).

> **4. Debts.** *All property directed to be distributed pursuant to the terms of this Article (other than property disposed of as part of the Residuary Trust Estate) shall be distributed subject to any lien, mortgage or other debt secured by such property. Otherwise, the Trustees in their sole discretion may (but shall not be obligated to) pay out of the trust estate any and all of my enforceable debts that are due and payable; provided, however, that no such debts shall be paid out of assets that are exempt from creditors' claims.*

The law in many states permits a fiduciary to distribute real estate and other collateralized property subject to the mortgage or other debt. However, a flat instruction to pay all debts would also require the trustee to pay off a mortgage or similar notes. The trust may not have sufficient liquidity, and paying the mortgage could either undermine the liquidity of the trust or force the sale of the real estate. Neither alternative may be in the best interest of the beneficiaries. With this clause, if a specific bequest of real estate (or other collateralized property, such as a car) is made, the beneficiary would take it subject to the mortgage or other debt, and would be responsible for payment of the mortgage debt thereafter. Real estate and other collateralized property that do pass as part of the residuary trust may pass subject to the mortgage or other debt, as the trustee determines to be appropriate.

The passing of the debt to the recipient of the collateralized property that is specifically devised or bequeathed is assumed to be the grantor's preference, because the beneficiaries of the residuary estate ordinarily should not bear responsibility for a liability related to property they will not receive. Also, payment of the debt may exhaust the residue, thus disinheriting the residuary takers. If the grantor intends to specifically devise real estate to a particular person, it is important to carefully review this provision and determine whether the grantor would prefer that the trust residue should pay the mortgage instead of the specified beneficiary.

The trustee is permitted to pay all other debts and claims against the grantor's estate out of the trust. The final subordinate clause of the last sentence is designed to emphasize the provision of the next clause to preserve tax- and creditor-exempt property.

> **5. *Prohibited Use of Property.*** *Notwithstanding any other provision of this section, the Trustees shall not use the proceeds of any qualified retirement plan or any property that is exempt from state or federal death taxes or the claims of other creditors that is held by or added to the trust estate by reason of my death to pay any debts, death taxes or expenses of administration pursuant to this section. The Trustees shall not contribute funds to my estate or make any payment directly or indirectly if such contribution or payment would subject to death taxes or the claims of other creditors property that otherwise would not be subject to such taxes or claims.*

This savings clause is primarily designed to preserve the tax status of estate tax-exempt assets. It also will protect creditor-exempt property, to some degree. As noted above, trust assets are subject to the claims of the grantor's creditors and are available to be used for the payment of the debts, expenses, and taxes of the grantor's estate. In many cases, grantors, on the advice of counsel, direct that their retirement accounts will be paid to their revocable trust at death. This allows the property to remain protected in continuing trust for the lifetime of the children, if that is desired. However, from an income tax perspective, this may be the equivalent of naming the estate as beneficiary if designation is not made properly. If the assets of the trust can be used to pay debts, taxes, and expenses, the retirement accounts would be treated as if the participant named his estate as the beneficiary. There are substantial adverse income tax results of that designation.[23] It is wisest to name not the revocable trust,

---

[23] Naming an estate as the beneficiary would require withdrawal of the assets from the account in a very short time, usually either one year or five years, depending on the age of the participant at death. This would force the early payment of the accumulated income taxes, which ordinarily should be avoided. An excellent resource with respect to the income tax implications of designating an estate or trust as beneficiary of a retirement account is Natalie Choate's *Life and Death Planning for Retirement Benefits,* sixth

generally, as the beneficiary of the retirement account, but the specific subtrust.[24] However, in the event these protective measures are overlooked in the planning stage, the language of this clause will save the retirement account from adverse income tax results by providing that any retirement assets that are added to the trust cannot be used to pay debts, taxes, and expenses.

In addition, if an asset would be exempt from estate taxes at the grantor's death, it must not be made available to pay the debts, taxes, or expenses of the grantor. If such exempt assets would be subject to claims or available for use to pay taxes or expense, the otherwise exempt property would become subject to death taxes in the grantor's estate. For example, the transfer of life insurance to an irrevocable life insurance trust is a common technique to avoid death tax liability on the proceeds. It is tempting to combine the life insurance trust with the revocable trust after the death of the grantor in order to increase administrative efficiency. However, if the insurance proceeds could be used to pay debts, taxes, or expenses, they will be subject to estate tax in the grantor's estate, despite the fact that they otherwise would have been exempt from death taxes.[25] Again, this clause is designed to avert that unfortunate result by prohibiting the use of such exempt property for the payment of debts, taxes, and expenses.

> **(B) *Cash Bequest.*** The Trustees shall distribute Fifty Thousand Dollars ($50,000) to my sister, Betty Roe, if

---

edition (Ataxplan Publications, 2006). It would be imprudent to name a trust as beneficiary of any retirement account without a thorough understanding of the estate tax and income tax consequences of such a designation. As estate tax exemptions grow, and as Americans invest more heavily in retirement accounts, income tax planning increasingly is becoming more important for most estate plans than is estate tax planning.

[24] As a practical matter, the beneficiary designation form itself should expressly provide that the retirement assets are specifically directed into the article that establishes the trust for the spouse or children, thus bypassing the trust provisions that permit the payment of debts, taxes, and expenses from trust property. A proper beneficiary designation form for a retirement account to name the trust for the children as beneficiary may use the following language: "The John J. Doe Revocable Trust dated 1/1/01, John J. Doe and Mary M. Doe, Trustees, to be disposed of pursuant to Article ___." Reference would be to the children's trust, which in the sample trust would be Article VI.

[25] Combining the insurance and revocable trust is possible and frequently done based on a discretionary power of the trustee or by directing revocable trust assets to the insurance trust after the settlement of all debts taxes and expenses.

> *she survives me, otherwise this bequest shall lapse [**or:** otherwise to her descendants who survive me, per stirpes].*

This clause is designed to make a bequest of a specified dollar amount. Ordinarily, this amount would be paid in cash, though it could be satisfied with specific assets if the trust lacks liquidity. To make a bequest of a specific asset, the following language might be used:

> **Specific Bequest.** *The Trustees shall distribute my diamond and sapphire necklace to my sister, Betty Roe, if she survives me, otherwise this bequest shall lapse [**or:** otherwise to her descendants who survive me, per stirpes]*

This alternative often is used with respect to the disposition of assets that may change in nature over time, such as stock in a business. In such cases, it is very important to carefully consider the language used. For example, if the grantor wishes to give 100 shares of stock in XYZ Inc. because he owns 100 shares of stock at the time the trust is drafted, what will happen if XYZ Inc. subsequently has a stock split and now his 100 shares become 200 shares? Will the beneficiary receive all 200 shares or just the 100 shares specifically identified in the agreement? In addition, another company could merge with XYZ Inc., and XYZ Inc. would no longer exist but the replacement stock of the successor company would exist. Would the specific beneficiary receive the successor stock? In making a bequest of stock, the following language may help to avoid any confusion:

> *My Trustees shall distribute all [or one-half or one-quarter] of my stock or other equity interest in XYZ, Inc., or any successor to such company, together with any accretions or reductions thereto, to . . .*

These sample clauses expressly state (as one option) that if the beneficiary does not survive the grantor, the bequest will lapse. State laws vary with respect to what happens to assets if the named beneficiary is not living. Most states have anti-lapse statutes, which provide that if a bequest is made in a will to certain individuals who are closely related to the decedent, the bequest will not lapse but will instead pass on to the descendants of the deceased beneficiary. For example, in most states a sister or brother is a sufficiently close relationship that the bequest would not lapse under the statute. A bequest of $100,000 to the grantor's brother, who predeceased the grantor, would pass to the brother's children unless the will otherwise specifies. This presumption is intended to apply only where the will is silent. Testamentary instructions in a will can override this presumption.

Anti-lapse statutes traditionally applied only to wills and not to trusts. However, with the increasing popularity of will substitutes, and in the face of a need to clarify ambiguous language, state law may extend the anti-lapse statutes to trusts as well as wills. Therefore. it is important to ensure that the language of the trust agreement is unequivocal in declaring how property will pass if the named beneficiary is deceased. If having the bequest survive in favor of the brother's children is the goal, the clause should specify "to my brother, if he survives me, otherwise to his descendants who survive me, *per stirpes*." If the bequest should not pass on to the brother's children, the clause should provide "to my brother, if he survives me, otherwise this bequest shall lapse."

A word of caution about the language "if he survives me": this phrase should be used only if the bequest is intended to be made immediately after the death of the grantor. If the bequest is intended to take effect at some later time, such as the death of the survivor of the grantor and his spouse, then the phrase "if he is then-living" should be used. In the later context, using the reference to survival of the grantor can create problems of interpretation. If the brother does survive the grantor, but does not survive the spouse, the question arises as to whether the property must be distributed to the brother's estate. A technical reading of the clause would require payment to the estate of the brother because he satisfied the condition of surviving the grantor. However, that interpretation may not be the intent of the testator. That misstatement creates a situation only a court can resolve. Quantifying the timing of distributions with the requirement of survival is important.

> **(C)** ***Devise of Real Property.*** *The Trustee shall distribute all of my real property [**or:** my real property located at 123 Main Street, Anytown, Anystate], together will all appurtenances thereto and buildings thereon, as well as any insurance policies related thereto, to my wife, if she survives me, otherwise this devise shall lapse.*

When the grantor desires to transfer real property to a specified individual, the language is somewhat different from the language of a bequest as used above. The term "devise" is used in the context of real property, whereas the term "bequest" is used in the context of personal property. In many cases, spouses instinctively believe they should leave their residence directly to their surviving spouse for convenience. Attorneys often agree that an outright distribution is the most convenient provision. In fact, making a specific devise of the real property to the spouse may ensure that the real estate will be the last asset sold to satisfy creditor claims.[26] Notwithstanding the convenience of a specific devise, there are significant tax benefits that may be derived, as well as creditor protections available, when the property is held in trust for the benefit of the spouse rather than held directly by the spouse. It is not always preferable to distribute the real estate directly to the surviving spouse.

If a specific devise of real estate to a spouse or to any beneficiary is contemplated, a thorough description of the property should include a full address or a deed description if an address is not available. In addition, the beneficiary should also be specifically bequeathed any insurance policy relating to the property. This will ensure that if the property is destroyed after the grantor's death but before distribution, the named beneficiary will receive the proceeds of that insurance policy. The provisions regarding the lapse for a deceased beneficiary apply with equal effect to the devise of real property as to bequests.

> **(D)** *Tangible Personal Property. The Trustees shall distribute all of the tangible personal property (except cash, currency, coins and bullion) held or received by the Trustees at the time of my death as follows:*
>
> > **1. Distributions.** *Such property shall be distributed to my wife, if my wife survives me. If my wife does not survive me, such property shall be divided among my*

---

[26] State law generally provides an order in which estate assets must be sold to satisfy claims. Assets in the residuary estate typically are the first to be sold. Specifically devised real estate often is the last to be sold. The use of a specific devise of real estate may protect the family home if an uncooperative administrator or trustee wished to sell the property to pay debts.

children who survive me, in such manner as they may agree. If my children cannot reach an agreement with respect to the disposition of such property within ninety (90) days after my death, or if any such child is then a minor or otherwise under a legal disability, then such property shall be divided by the Trustees in as nearly equal shares as practicable.

2. ***Claims, Costs and Instructions.*** Each beneficiary of tangible personal property under this section shall be entitled to any claims in my favor existing at my death with respect to the property distributed to such beneficiary, and, to the extent practical, shall be entitled to any insurance policies (or the proceeds of such policy if such proceeds become payable after my death) relating to such tangible personal property. Any costs of distribution of any tangible personal property, including, without limitation, storage, insurance, packing and delivery, shall be paid out of my general estate as an administrative expense. It is my request, without creating any legal obligation, that my Executors and family give due consideration to any separate instructions left by me for their guidance with respect to dividing and disposing of my tangible personal property.

Tangible personal property includes all of those assets that are not real estate or intangible personal property. Intangible personal property includes cash, notes, bonds, stock, and similar items. Therefore, tangible personal property refers to items such as clothing, jewelry, artwork, household furnishings, personal effects, automobiles, boats, campers, and items of that nature. The term can refer to items of virtually no value, such as an old couch or clothes, as well as priceless antiques and collectibles. It is important to consider the nature and value of the tangible personal property before simply adopting a blanket disposition of the grantor's tangible personal property as provided by this clause. If specific items of tangible personal property are to pass to specific beneficiaries, the "specific devise" clause indicated in the preceding section should be used.

In addition to inanimate objects, pets ordinarily would be considered tangible personal property and would be disposed of under the terms of this clause. This includes livestock and breeding animals as well, unless they are owned in a separate business entity. For those who wish to make special disposition of their pets, they should incorporate a special clause relating to that.[27]

In most cases, the beneficiaries of the tangible personal property are the same as the beneficiaries of the residuary trust estate (discussed in Article V below). It may seem unnecessary to carve out a description of tangible personal property and distribute it to the same beneficiaries who will receive all other property, and it is tempting to dispense with this tangible personal property clause. Doing so is not advisable for two reasons. The first is merely practical. The language of this clause permits the beneficiaries the opportunity to decide among themselves how this property will be distributed. If this clause deals primarily with personal items of limited value, this will save time and energy in the settlement process. Of course, the trustee is given final say to arbitrate any disputes among the beneficiaries, but if they can agree, it is simply easier to allow them to do so, particularly if the primary factor is the sentimental value rather than the fair market value of the items.

The second reason is, of course, tax-driven. The relevant tax in this case is not the estate tax, but income tax. During the administration of the trust after the death of the grantor, the trust is an independent income tax payer. Any income earned in the trust is subject to income tax. However, if property is distributed to a beneficiary, income of the trust is carried out to the beneficiary in an amount equal to the lesser of the value of the property or the amount of income. For example, if the trust has income of $20,000, and the beneficiary receives a trust distribution valued at $30,000, the trust will pay no income tax, but the beneficiary will be treated as receiving $20,000 of income and will be obligated to pay the income tax liability on that amount of income. One exception to this general rule is if the property

---

[27] See Appendix B for some sample language that can be used for distribution of a pet.

Line-by-Line Analysis 57

distributed to the beneficiary is a specific bequest.[28] If the tangible personal property passes to the beneficiaries as part of the residuary trust estate, income will be carried out to the beneficiaries. Because of the nature of the property, the beneficiary may have a substantial tax bill, but no liquid assets with which to pay the tax. By making a specific distribution of the tangible personal property, as done in this clause, the exception to the general rule applies and the beneficiary is not treated as receiving income when he receives the tangible personal property.

This clause provides that the costs of storing, shipping, and otherwise dealing with tangible personal property should be borne by the trust as an administration expense, and not by the individual beneficiaries. This language is necessary to ensure that these costs are deductible for estate tax purposes, as discussed with respect to the payment of debts, taxes, and expenses. Local law varies as to whether such costs are the responsibility of the beneficiary or the trust. If they are the responsibility of the beneficiary, they are not deductible for estate tax purposes. This clause (like all of the other provisions of this section expressing that an expense should be paid as "an expense of administration") will allow the expense to be deductible regardless of what local law otherwise provides. Of course, the corollary of that is the obligation of the trust to bear those costs. The grantor should carefully consider what those costs may be, whether trust payment of those costs would be disproportionately beneficial to one or more of the beneficiaries, and whether estate taxes are a consideration with respect to the trust before adopting language of this nature.

Any insurance policy associated with tangible personal property, such as motor vehicle insurance or homeowners insurance riders, should pass with the property to the beneficiary. This will enable the beneficiary to receive the benefits of the insurance proceeds if the property is destroyed prior to receipt.

---

[28] The income taxation of trusts is set forth in Subchapter J of Chapter 1 of the Internal Revenue Code, §641 et. seq. The rules are complex, and there are a variety of exceptions. A professional tax accountant or tax attorney should be consulted when such issues arise. There are, however, some excellent tax treaties on the subject. See, e.g., Howard M. Zaritsky and Norman H. Lane, *Federal Income Taxation of Estate and Trusts* (Warren Gorham & Lamont/RIA, 2003).

Finally, this clause requests that the trustee consult any memorandum that the grantor may leave separately indicating specific wishes with respect to the disposition of tangible personal property. For example, the grantor may express that the family silver should be given to one child and the china to another child and the jewelry to yet another child. In most states, these memoranda are not legally binding, but they do provide input to the trustee and family when making decisions about how various assets of tangible personal property should be distributed. In states where a memorandum of this nature is legally binding, such as Florida, a more formal expression of intent to rely on the memorandum should be used.

It is not unusual for the disposition of family heirlooms and items of tangible personal property to be at least as contentious as other assets of substantially greater value. Therefore, it is important if there are specific wishes relating to disposition of this property that they be written down and kept with the trust document. If there are provisions the grantor considers imperative, or if there is a potential for disputes over distribution, those provisions should be written directly into the trust instrument. Inclusion in the trust agreement makes the distribution provision mandatory rather than merely advisory.

> **(E) *Disposition of Residuary Trust Estate.*** *The balance of the trust estate not otherwise disposed of by the preceding provisions of this Agreement and expressly including any lapsed or failed bequest or devise, (the "Residuary Trust Estate") shall be disposed of pursuant to Article IV of this Agreement.*

The distribution of the remaining trust property clause is the final provision of the post-death administrative clauses. It directs that after the payment of all debts, taxes, expenses, and the disposition of specific property as indicated in the preceding clauses, all of the rest of the trust property will be distributed as provided in the following article. This is known as the residuary trust estate in the same manner that it would be called the residuary estate under a will. The actual terminology used to identify the remaining trust property is not particularly important. However, the residuary trust estate is referred to in several places throughout the instrument, and it is important that it have a name for ease of reference.

Line-by-Line Analysis 59

Article V

Article V sets forth the disposition of trust property for a married couple when the first spouse dies. If the grantor is not married, this article would be inapplicable. Article VI would simply move up to become Article V. The language of this article is intended to be used when the grantor desires to take advantage of basic estate tax planning strategies that are available to married couples. Where the grantor's estate is too small to warrant tax planning, these complex clauses are not required.[29] As a brief overview, Sections A and B set forth the provisions with respect to a surviving spouse. Section C sets forth the disposition of property if the spouse predeceases the grantor. They allow the grantor to take advantage of the exemption from both federal and state estate tax laws, as well as the federal and state marital deductions.

Before engaging in a line-by-line analysis of the clauses in this article, it is important to have a background understanding of relevant tax rules and the basic tax planning engaged in for couples.[30] It is fairly common knowledge that there may be substantial taxes imposed when a person dies, and that there are ways to mitigate those taxes through proper estate planning. The federal "wealth transfer tax" is a generic term that encompasses three separate, but related, tax regimes. These regimes include the gift tax, the estate tax (sometimes derisively called the "death tax"), and the GST tax. Although these are distinct tax regimes that are imposed at different times and for different reasons, the one thing they share in common is that they all impose a tax on the giver for the privilege of transferring his or her wealth to another.

---

[29] The decision to avoid including tax savings clauses in a revocable living trust, even for small estates, should be done only after careful consideration. The failure to include tax planning, or at least discussing the option with the client, may be malpractice for any attorney, even where the current assets or tax law would not merit tax planning because the client's assets could grow or the tax exemptions could change and the grantor may no longer be capable of making the necessary changes. Appendix B contains a clause permitting outright distribution to the surviving spouse, while allowing for the creation of a trust by disclaimer, which may be used for smaller estates where tax planning may not be required, but is incorporated as a failsafe measure.

[30] Portions of this introduction are adapted from client advisories prepared by the author for clients of the law firm of Halloran and Sage LLP in Hartford, Connecticut, and they are used with permission.

The Gift Tax

The federal gift tax is implicated when an individual makes a transfer during their lifetime. An individual is permitted under IRC §2503(b) to give up to $10,000 per year, adjusted for inflation, to anyone without incurring a gift tax. This right is commonly referred to as the annual exclusion from gift tax. The annual exclusion amount is indexed for inflation and may increase by $1,000 every few years.[31] If the giver of the gift, usually called the donor, is married, he or she may gift twice the annual exclusion amount, to any individual each year. However, the donor's spouse must file a gift tax return on which he or she consents to allow the donor spouse to use the non-donor spouse's annual exclusion gifting privilege. By doing so, the non-donor spouse relinquishes his or her right to use that annual exclusion for that year for that beneficiary. If assets are gifted from a joint account, or if each spouse makes separate gifts that do not exceed the annual exclusion amount, it is not necessary to file a gift tax return.[32]

Over the course of a lifetime, each person may give away the cumulative amount of $1 million, in addition to annual exclusion gifts, without paying federal gift tax. After the $1 million has been gifted, a tax is imposed on each gift in excess of that amount. The tax is due by April 15 of the year following the year in which the gift is made. The tax is paid by the donor, the person who makes the gift, not the person who receives the gift. The federal gift tax currently is imposed at a flat rate of 45 percent after the $1 million exemption is exhausted. While the federal government imposes a gift tax, each state also may impose a separate gift tax. Many states do not impose gift taxes, and those that do have different schemes. It is important to review each state's gift tax laws.

---

[31] As of 2008, the inflation adjustment increased the gift amount to $12,000. The rules relating to the gift tax are set forth in Chapter 12 of the IRC §2501, et. seq.

[32] There are certain types of gifts that are not treated as gifts and do not use any portion of the annual exclusion. Under IRC §2503(e), these include tuition payments on behalf of another person so long as they are paid directly to the educational institution. This is limited to tuition and does not include room and board, books, or other fees. Medical payments made directly to a health care provider also are not treated as gifts. This means a grandparent can pay for a grandchild's uninsured medical expense (such as dental bills). It also includes the payment of premiums for medical insurance on behalf of another person.

Line-by-Line Analysis

The Estate Tax

The federal estate tax is a tax imposed when assets are transferred as a result of a person's death, thus earning it the ignominious title of the death tax.[33] Modern estate tax law provides an exemption over a certain amount of assets passing at death. This exemption is found in IRC §2010. This estate tax exemption amount is commonly referred to as the "unified credit amount" or the "lifetime exemption amount," though the technical term currently used by the code is the "applicable exclusion amount." However, as a matter of convenience here, the term "exemption" or "lifetime exemption" is used throughout when discussing the amount that can pass free of estate tax under IRC §2010. If a person used any portion of his or her $1 million gift tax exemption during their lifetime, the estate tax exemption amount available at death is reduced by the amount of gift tax exemption used.

Congress periodically passes major transfer tax reforms. The most recent reform legislation, passed in 2001, is known as the Economic Growth and Tax Relief Reconciliation Act. Prior to adoption of the act, the federal estate and gift tax both had an exemption of $1 million, with a tax imposed at a progressive rate ranging from 18 percent up to 55 percent, with a surtax of an additional 5 percent on estates over $10 million. The act was designed to gradually reduce the rate of tax to a flat rate of 45 percent for all estates and increase the lifetime exemption amount to $3,5 million by 2009. It also completely repealed the estate tax for the year 2010.[34] The act provides that

---

[33] The rules relating to the estate tax are set forth in Chapter 11 of the IRC §2001, et. seq.

[34] The following chart summarizes the tax rates under the Economic Growth and Tax Relief Reconciliation Act:

Year	Estate and Generation-Skipping Transfer Tax Exemption	Maximum Estate Tax Rate	Gift Tax Exemption	Maximum Gift Tax Rate
2003	$1,000,000	49%	$1,000,000	49%
2004	$1,500,000	48%	$1,000,000	48%
2005	$1,500,000	47%	$1,000,000	47%
2006	$2,000,000	46%	$1,000,000	46%
2007	$2,000,000	45%	$1,000,000	45%
2008	$2,000,000	45%	$1,000,000	45%

the federal estate and gift tax pre-2001 rules will be reinstated in 2011 for all future years with an exemption amount equal to $1 million and graduated rates up to 55 or 60 percent.[35]

In addition to the lifetime exemption, the federal estate and gift tax regimes also provide for an unlimited deduction for assets passing to a surviving spouse.[36] This is known as the marital deduction. Any assets left directly to a surviving spouse (who is a citizen of the United States[37]) at death, or gifted to a spouse during lifetime, pass free of estate or gift taxes. If the transferred assets are to be held in trust for a spouse, rather than distributed outright to the spouse, there are certain strict requirements that must be met in order for the assets in trust to qualify for the martial deduction.

2009	$3,500,000	45%	$1,000,000	45%
2010*	N/A	N/A	$1,000,000	35%
2011**	$1,000,000	55%***	$1,000,000	55%

* Estate tax is repealed for one year, capital gains treatment for transfers at death; gift tax remains with an exemption of $1 million, gift tax rate equals top income tax rate.
** Estate, gift, and GST tax reinstated with exemptions equivalent to 2001 schedules; inflation adjustments provide moderate increase in GST tax exemption. Rates and exemption for 2011 apply for all successive years.
*** An additional 5 percent surtax is imposed on large estates over $10 million, raising the rate to 60 percent.

[35] Although this "sunset" provision seems to be yet another act of legislators gone wild, there is some method to their madness. Legislative rules prohibit the Senate from passing a law that will have a revenue impact greater than a certain dollar amount with less than a supermajority. Because the proponents of estate tax reform could not garner sufficient votes to reach the threshold supermajority, the act had to sunset after 2010 or the revenue impact would be too great. Proponents expected to gain sufficient support over time to make the changes permanent, but to date have been unsuccessful in doing so. Most specialists who are knowledgeable about tax matters and the legislative process do not expect that this proposed regime will survive. The current prevailing expectation is that the estate and gift tax will not be repealed entirely. The looming question remains what the lifetime exemption amount and rate of tax will be.

[36] The law also provides for an unlimited deduction for amounts passing to qualified charity. However, a discussion of those rules is beyond the scope of this text.

[37] There are limits on the amount that can pass to a spouse who is not a citizen of the United States. If the surviving spouse is not a U.S. citizen, assets must be held in a special trust, commonly referred to as a qualified domestic trust, under IRC §2056A in order for the marital deduction to be available.

Line-by-Line Analysis

These requirements are discussed in the analysis of the relevant clauses below.

The premise of the marital deduction is that the assets accumulated by a couple during their lifetime should be available to support the couple until both are deceased. If approximately 50 percent of the couple's assets are lost to taxes at the death of the first to die, the standard of living of the surviving spouse would be severely diminished. The government is willing to wait until the second death to collect taxes on the assets that remain.

Many states also impose a separate tax to be imposed on transfers at death. Prior to 2001, the federal government shared estate tax revenue with the states by providing a credit under IRC §2011 to an estate for the amounts paid as state death taxes up to approximately 17 percent. States adopted laws to collect that amount, and the estate was in no worse a position because if it did not pay that amount to the state government, it would have paid that amount to the federal government. With the passage of the Economic Growth and Tax Relief Reconciliation Act, Congress did away with this revenue-sharing mechanism. As a result, states stood to lose a significant amount of revenue. In response, many states adopted their own estate tax rules that were no longer tied to the federal system.[38] This divorcing of the state systems from the federal rules is commonly referred to as "de-coupling." As a result of de-coupling, it is now necessary to plan to take advantage of both the federal exemption and the state exemption, if any.[39]

---

[38] As a consequence, many estates now will pay considerably more tax than they did before 2001 by paying at least 45 percent of the estate to the federal government and 16 percent to the state government. The cumulative tax may be as high as 61 percent, where it previously had been limited to 55 percent (or 60 percent for very large estates). Even if the federal estate tax ultimately is repealed, the state estate tax regimes are certain to perpetuate the need for tax planning with respect to the transfer of wealth at death.

[39] In states that have no separate estate tax, or where the state and federal exemptions are the same, it is not necessary to distinguish between the state and federal exemption amounts. However, it is always possible that the state could adopt a separate estate tax, or that the state could de-couple. It may be worthwhile to include the distinction in such cases in order to avoid the need to amend the trust at some future date in the event there is such a change.

The GST Tax

The final tax regime directly related to estate planning is known as the GST tax. In its simplest terms, this tax imposes an additional transfer tax when property passes, in any fashion, from a grandparent to a grandchild. Obviously, the terms of the law are much broader, but the grandparent-grandchild transfer is the classic scenario the law is designed to address.[40]

The federal government would prefer to collect an estate tax at the passing of each generation. No surprise there. If a transfer skips a generation by passing directly from a grandparent to a grandchild, the government loses the opportunity to impose a transfer tax at the death of the child. In lieu of the estate tax that would have been imposed at the death of the child, the GST tax is imposed on the transfer, in addition to either a gift or estate tax imposed on the donor.[41] The tax applies not only to direct transfers from grandparent to grandchild, called a direct skip transfer, but also to transfers from trusts that are either taxable distributions or taxable terminations (as those terms are defined in IRC §§2611–2613). If the transferor of the trust property is a grandparent (or the generational equivalent) of the beneficiary who receives either an interim distribution from the trust or who receives a final distribution upon termination of the trust, the GST tax will apply. If the trust is exempt from the GST tax because it qualified for the grantor's GST tax exemption, then no tax liability is imposed. If the trust is not exempt because the value of the trust was greater than the grantor's available exemption, the GST tax will be imposed at a flat rate of 45 percent of the amount distributed.[42]

---

[40] Specifically, the tax applies to any time property passes to a transferee who is two or more generations junior to the transferor as defined in IRC §2651. It applies to any such generational relationship, including grandparents, great-uncles, and the like. If there is no relationship between the parties to the transfer, either by blood or marriage, the law looks to the age of the parties. If the transferee is more than thirty-seven and a half years younger than the transferor, the transferee will be deemed to be two generations junior to the transferor and the tax will apply. The rules relating to the GST tax are set forth in Chapter 13 of the IRC, §2601, et. seq.

[41] The scope of this book necessarily deals only with the interrelation of the estate tax and the GST tax. However, it should be noted that the GST tax also applies to multi-generational lifetime transfers by gift.

[42] When the GST tax applies, it is imposed at the highest estate tax rate. Historically, the estate tax was imposed at a graduated rate based on the value of the estate. The GST tax

As with the estate tax, each person has a lifetime exemption from the GST tax. Under current law, the GST tax exemption is equal to the estate tax exemption. If the law reverts to pre-2001 rules after 2010, the GST tax exemption will be $1 million plus annual adjustments for inflation. Since the $1 million estate tax exemption under pre-2001 law was not adjusted for inflation, the exemptions would not be the same. The exemption allows each individual to pass the exemption amount directly to a grandchild either during lifetime or at death. More common, however, is the option of holding the exemption amount in a trust for the benefit of children. In this way, the property is available to children, if it is needed by them during their lifetimes. However, if the children do not use the property during their lifetimes, it can pass on to their children (i.e., the grantor's grandchildren) free from all estate, gift, and GST taxes. For this reason, many people elect to leave at least the GST tax exemption amount in a lifetime trust for their children, even if there is no other compelling reason to use a trust rather than a direct inheritance.

Tax Planning for a Basic Estate Plan

As indicated, each person is entitled to an exemption from estate tax up to a certain amount, which may vary over time. In addition, each person may leave an unlimited amount to his or her spouse free of estate taxes. Unfortunately, the lifetime exemption and marital deduction are mutually exclusive. Any amount left to a spouse that qualifies for the marital deduction does not qualify for the lifetime exemption. Most couples prefer to leave all of their assets to the surviving spouse so they can be available for his or her needs. Doing so, however, wastes the lifetime exemption of the first spouse to die. This results in the couple protecting only the exemption amount available to the surviving spouse at death, rather than twice that amount.

---

was imposed at a flat rate of 55 percent, regardless of value. The GST tax is imposed in addition to the estate tax, potentially reducing the net transfer to a mere fraction of the original amount. For example, a transfer of $100,000 that was fully subject to both taxes may be reduced to $55,000 by the 45 percent estate tax and again to $24,750 by the GST tax. Since 2006 (following passage of the Economic Growth and Tax Relief Reconciliation Act in 2001), the estate tax is no longer imposed at a graduated rate based on value. Rather, both the estate tax and the GST tax are imposed at a flat rate of 45 percent.

Proper drafting allows a couple to ensure that all of the assets are available to the surviving spouse, yet still preserve the estate tax exemption of the first spouse to die. Rather than leaving all of the assets outright to the survivor, the first spouse to die can leave the exemption amount to a trust for the benefit of the spouse and, if desired, children. This type of trust is referred to by many names in estate planning literature, including the credit shelter trust, credit trust, exemption trust, family trust, and bypass trust.

The credit shelter trust should be drafted flexibly so the surviving spouse has access to income and principal. The spouse may even act as a trustee. In addition, descendants may be added as potential beneficiaries of the trust so distributions can be made to them free of transfer taxes if the surviving spouse's needs are otherwise adequately met. When the surviving spouse dies, the assets remaining in the trust, including all growth in the assets, pass on free of estate tax. The survivor also has his or her own exemption amount that will pass free of tax. In this manner, a couple effectively can pass twice the exemption amount to descendants free of estate tax rather than just one exemption amount. Because the rate of tax is almost 50 percent, this technique will save estate taxes equal to approximately one-half of the value of the exemption.

The assets in excess of the lifetime exemption amount may be left outright to the surviving spouse, or they may be left in a special trust for the benefit of the spouse. The tax consequences of this decision generally are neutral (except with respect to the ability to make adequate state tax elections in decoupled states, as discussed below). That is to say, the assets will qualify for the marital deduction regardless of whether they pass outright or in a qualified trust. The decision to use a trust to qualify for the marital deduction typically is one of control by the grantor, not tax savings.

Assets left directly to the surviving spouse automatically qualify for the estate tax marital deduction. Assets left in a properly drafted trust that grants a general power of appointment to the spouse also automatically qualify for the marital deduction under IRC §2056(b)(5).[43] The general

---

[43] The government is assured of its ability to tax the assets in the general power of appointment trust because a general power of appointment causes the value of the trust will be included in the spouse's estate under IRC §2041. Because the general power of

power of appointment allows the spouse to appoint trust property to any person, including herself, her estate, or the creditors of either. Such a broad power may not be desirable if the grantor's beneficiaries are different from those his spouse would prefer to benefit, as may be the case when there are children of a prior marriage. This broad general power of appointment provides no control to the grantor, because the surviving spouse has ultimate control over how the assets will be distributed at the death of the survivor.

To establish a trust that will qualify for the marital deduction and still allow the grantor to maintain ultimate control over distribution, the trust must meet the requirements of a qualified terminable interest property trust, known by its acronym as a QTIP trust, under IRC §2056(b)(7). Although this type of trust *can* qualify for the marital deduction, it does not automatically do so. Rather, the grantor's executor must make an appropriate election on the estate tax return filed with respect to the grantor's estate opting to qualify for the marital deduction. This rule provides significant flexibility by allowing the executor to take a second look and make critical tax decisions at the grantor's death. The assets in a QTIP trust ordinarily would not be subject to estate tax under any of the usual estate tax statutes. When the power to create a QTIP trust was first enacted, Congress also enacted IRC §2044, whereby an election made to qualify a QTIP trust for the marital deduction is an election to allow the assets remaining in the trust at the death of the surviving spouse to be taxed in the estate of the survivor. The government is thus assured of having an opportunity to tax these assets at the death of the surviving spouse. This is the critical tax distinction between the credit shelter trust and the marital trust. The former trust will not be subject to estate tax when the surviving spouse dies, but the later will be. Therefore, the tax objective always is to maximize the amount that will qualify for the lifetime exemption as opposed to the marital deduction.

The decision of whether to use a martial trust becomes an important tax decision if the federal exemption amount and the state exemption amount are different, as with the so-called de-coupled states. In those states, it may be necessary to have a martial trust for the first spouse to die to take

---

appointment trust is rarely used, it is not discussed in this book. There are other treatises that discuss this trust option in greater detail.

maximum advantage of the federal exemption, while still avoiding any state estate tax at the first death. The outright distribution to a spouse and the use of a general power of appointment trust (as provided by IRC §2056(b)(5)) have inherent limitations with respect to tax planning. Both an outright distribution and a general power of appointment trust automatically qualify for the marital deduction. Unlike the QTIP trust, the executor of the grantor's estate does not have the flexibility to decide after death whether to qualify all or a portion of the trust for the lifetime exemption instead of the marital deduction. This flexibility is particularly important in de-coupled states where the state exemption is less than the federal exemption. In such states, a QTIP trust can be used to take full advantage of the federal exemption (by not electing to qualify for the marital deduction) while still qualifying for the state marital deduction and avoiding all state taxes at the death of the grantor. Since the general power of appointment trust automatically qualifies for the marital deduction, it cannot be used to take advantage of the federal lifetime exemption. For this reason, grantors should give serious consideration to using a martial trust as a tax-saving strategy even where it otherwise may not be necessary.

The following example will illustrate the manner in which a QTIP trust will work in de-coupled states to maximize the federal exemption while avoiding state taxes. Assume the grantor is married and he has a net estate of $5 million. The federal exemption is $3.5 million but the state exemption is only $1 million. A properly drafted trust would provide that the credit shelter trust is funded with the maximum amount that can pass free of both state and federal taxes. Since the maximum that can pass free of state taxes is $1 million, this trust will necessary be limited to $1 million. The remaining $4 million will pass to the marital trust. This avoids any state tax at the grantor's death. However, there is an additional $2.5 million of federal exemption that is essentially wasted because it was added to the marital trust. To prevent this waste, the marital trust should be divided into two trusts. One, Trust A, would be funded with $2.5 million. The other, Trust B, would be funded with the remaining $1,5 million. With respect to Trust B, the executor would elect to qualify it for both the state and federal marital deduction. With respect to Trust A, the executor would elect to qualify the trust for the state marital deduction in order to avoid state taxes, and would not elect to qualify for the federal marital deduction, thereby taking advantage of the remaining available federal exemption. Thus, Trust

B would be subject to both state and federal taxes in the survivor's estate. Trust A would be subject to state tax, but not federal tax at the death of the survivor. The credit shelter trust would not be subject to either state or federal tax at the death of the survivor.[44]

For a trust to qualify for the marital deduction, it is essential that it meet certain requirements under IRC §2056(b)(7). Some of these requirements, which are discussed in more detail in the line-by-line analysis of Section B of this article, include the requirement that the trust must provide that the surviving spouse is the sole beneficiary for life. The spouse cannot cease to be a beneficiary for any reason. For example, the trust cannot provide that the spouse will cease to be a beneficiary in the event of remarriage. Even if the spouse never remarried, such language would cause the trust to fail to qualify for the marital deduction. Also, all of the income of the trust must be distributed to the spouse each year. Principal may be distributed to the spouse, but it is not required.

The language of the sample trust is designed to create a credit shelter trust under Section A that will be funded with the maximum exemption under both state and federal tax laws. Older trusts and form books refer only to the maximum amount that can pass free of federal estate tax, without reference to the amount that can pass free of state death tax, because the state and federal exemptions were the same prior to the Economic Growth and Tax Relief Reconciliation Act. The amount in excess of the exemption is added to a marital QTIP trust under Section B.

---

[44] Before engaging in this type of planning, it is important to review state tax law. Theoretically it is possible to elect to qualify a marital trust for the marital deduction under state law, but not federal law, thus allowing the trust to qualify for the federal lifetime exemption and the state marital deduction. However, some states prohibit the making of separate state and federal elections regarding the marital trust. In those decoupled states, this plan would not work. In some states, it may work if Trust A is a marital trust while the assets that would have passed to Trust B pass outright to the spouse instead. In other cases where the use of a marital trust for control is essential, it may be worthwhile to pay a smaller state tax at the first death by funding the credit shelter trust with the maximum federal exemption in order to take maximum advantage of the greater federal tax savings. All of these options will need to be considered in light of the governing law and the grantor's objectives in each case.

Article V. *Disposition of Residuary Trust Estate.*

The property to be disposed of pursuant to this Article shall be disposed of as follows:

(A) **Credit Shelter Share.** *If my wife survives me, the Trustees shall set aside the largest fractional share of the Residuary Trust Estate that may pass free of both federal estate tax and any state death tax imposed by reason of my death (referred to herein as the "Credit Shelter Share"), which share shall be determined and disposed of as follows:*

1. **Determination of Credit Shelter Share.** *For purposes of this section, the largest fractional share of the Residuary Trust Estate that may pass free of federal estate tax imposed by reason of my death (the "federal credit share") shall be determined based only on the credit against estate taxes provided by section 2010 of the Code and the credit for state death taxes under section 2011 of the Code, if applicable, but only to the extent that it does not increase the death tax payable to any state. It shall be calculated by using the final determinations in the federal estate tax proceeding for my estate. The largest fractional share of the Residuary Trust Estate that will pass free of any state death tax imposed by reason of my death (the "state credit share") shall be determined by using the final determinations in each applicable state death tax proceeding for my estate. The term "state death tax" shall not include any generation-skipping transfer tax imposed by any state. In calculating either the federal credit share or the state credit share, each shall be calculated by deducting the amount of any such credit (including any credit for gift tax purposes) used by me during lifetime and by the amount of any such credit applied against property passing pursuant to any prior provision of this Agreement or outside if this Agreement, and assuming that the balance of the*

> *Residuary Trust Estate qualifies for any marital deduction or exemption allowed by section 2056 of the Code or by any similar provision of any such state, regardless of whether all or any portion of it does in fact so qualify. There shall be allocated to the share to be disposed of under this section any property that would not qualify for the federal estate tax marital deduction or any applicable state death tax marital deduction or exemption if allocated to the Residuary Marital Share.*

This clause establishes the formula used to create the credit shelter trust. It is designed to fund the trust with a fractional share of the total residuary estate equal to the maximum amount that can pass free of both state and federal tax.[45] This language is designed to address the issue of de-coupling, as discussed above. The residuary trust estate is a defined term in the final section of the preceding article, and it essentially means the entire trust property remaining after payment of debts, taxes, expenses, and pre-residuary bequests. The value of the assets are based on the value of the estate as finally determined for the state and federal estate tax proceedings for the estate of the grantor. This is necessary so the formula will be self-adjusting if the values are changed by the tax authorities after an audit of the tax returns. The exclusion of the GST tax from the definition of state death taxes is necessary because it may or may not be a tax imposed by the states and this clause is not designed to address the implications of the GST tax. It is not necessary to distinguish the GST tax for federal purposes because the estate and GST taxes are two separate regimes under federal tax law.

The only credit applicable to the determination of the maximum federal exemption is the exemption amount provided in IRC §2010 and the state

---

[45] There are at least seven different formulas that can be used to create the division between the credit share and the marital share. A discussion of all of these formulas would constitute a book in and of itself. The fractional funding formula employed here is becoming the most popular, but other practitioners prefer other options. There are circumstances where other formulas could achieve greater tax savings based on post-death appreciation of assets. For a thorough analysis of the benefits and risks of the various funding formulae, see Sebastian V. Grassi Jr.'s *A Practical Guide to Drafting Marital Deduction Trusts* (ALI-ABA, 2004), especially Chapters 15 and 17.

death tax credit under IRC §2011. Under the Economic Growth and Tax Relief Reconciliation Act, there no longer is a state death tax credit, but reference to the credit remains because of the impending sunset of the rules. The state death tax credit can only be used to the extent it will not cause an increase in the state death taxes payable. To determine the amount that will pass free of all taxes under IRC §2010 (i.e., the exemption amount), it is necessary to assume that the entire balance will qualify for the marital deduction. In that way, application of the exemption amount to the credit shelter trust, plus the marital deduction available for the balance, will reduce the estate tax liability for the estate to zero.

Once the amount of the total exemption is determined under both state and federal law, the allowable exemption is reduced by any prior use of exemption in order to determine the available exemption. Prior use of exemption may have occurred by lifetime gifts or by transfers made at death to someone other than the grantor's spouse. These would have occurred either under the preceding articles (such as a cash bequest to a child) or outside of the instrument (such as by naming a sibling as the beneficiary of a retirement account or insurance policy). The formula also requires that any property that would not qualify for the marital deduction, such as certain annuities or other terminating interests, must be added to the credit shelter trust rather than the marital trust.

> 2. ***Distributions.*** *The Trustees shall hold the Credit Shelter Share in a separate trust hereunder (called the "Credit Shelter Trust") and may distribute so much or all of the net income and principal thereof to such one or more members of the class of individuals consisting of my wife and those of my descendants who are living from time to time during the term of the trust, in such shares and proportions, without requirement of equality, as the Trustees consider advisable to provide for the education, maintenance in health and reasonable comfort, and support in accustomed manner of living of any one or more of such individuals. In addition, the Independent Trustee may distribute so much or all of the net income and principal thereof to such one or more members of said*

> *class, in such shares and proportions, without requirement of equality, as the Independent Trustee considers advisable in its sole, absolute and uncontrolled discretion for any purposes whatsoever. The Trustees shall accumulate and add to principal at least annually any net income not so paid.*

After the trust is established and funded pursuant to the preceding subsection, the balance of the clauses in this section set forth the terms for administration of the trust. This Subsection 2 establishes the terms upon which distributions can be made. The clause identifies the beneficiaries as the surviving spouse and all descendants. The trustee is given fairly broad discretion to make distributions to meet the needs of these beneficiaries for their health, education, and support in accustomed manner of living. For the reasons discussed earlier with respect to the provisions of Article III, distributions are limited by an ascertainable standard in the event a beneficiary is acting as trustee. In most cases, the surviving spouse can and will be a trustee of the credit shelter trust. If she is, it is necessary to limit distributions to an ascertainable standard in order to prevent this trust from being included in her estate.

The ascertainable standard is very broad and should meet most family needs that arise. However, it is possible that family members may desire a distribution that would not fit within the terms of health, education, or support. For example, the spouse may desire to take an extended trip around the world. That really does not fit within any of the categories for distribution unless her lifestyle customarily lends itself to trips around the world. This clause would permit an independent trustee to make distributions for any purpose without the restrictions of an ascertainable standard.[46] The family may appoint an independent trustee if one is needed, but otherwise the spouse may act as sole trustee so long as no extraordinary distributions are required.

For most married grantors, the primary goal is to provide for their spouse during his or her lifetime and to delay providing for children until both spouses are deceased. In light of that, many credit shelter trusts often

---

[46] For a discussion relating to independent trustees, see the analysis of Section G of Article I.

permit distributions only to the spouse. While this is not wrong, it can be unduly limiting. If the surviving spouse is the only beneficiary, there is no flexibility in making transfers to other family members. If a descendant needs money, or if the spouse wants to make a transfer to a descendant, the spouse must make a gift, which may be subject to the gift tax, in order to get money to the descendant. If, instead, the descendant is a permitted beneficiary of the credit shelter trust, distributions can be made to the descendant without gift tax implications. If there is a likelihood that the descendants may fight with the spouse over distributions, as may be the case where the children are from a prior marriage or where a child has addiction problems, it may be preferable to exclude the children as current beneficiaries of the credit shelter trust in order to protect the spouse.

Another popular restriction on the credit shelter trust is to require that all of the income be distributed to the surviving spouse each year. The language would be identical to the marital trust language in Section B of this article. However, as discussed, the benefit of this trust is that it can pass entirely free of state and federal estate taxes after the death of the surviving spouse. A provision requiring distribution of all income could undermine this benefit. If the spouse does not need the income, such a clause would force out the income and would unnecessarily diminish the trust. Also, it may be preferable to pass the income to the children rather than the spouse if the spouse does not need the income and giving it to her will only increase her estate tax liability. From an income tax perspective, it may be desirable to have all income pass out to the beneficiaries, but the trustee can do so in his discretion rather than making it mandatory. A better alternative may be to invest the trust assets in growth property rather than income-producing property to avoid income taxes payable by the trust or the beneficiaries.

> 3. ***Limitation on Distributions.*** *It is my request, without creating any legal obligation, that notwithstanding the foregoing no discretionary payment should be made from the principal of this trust to my wife unless and until all of the principal of the Marital Trust under section (B) of this Article has been completely paid out. The Trustees shall give first consideration to the needs of my wife before making*

> *distributions of income or principal of this trust to other eligible beneficiaries.*

As indicated previously, the assets remaining in the credit shelter trust will pass free of estate taxes at the death of the surviving spouse. As such, it is intended that the surviving spouse will exhaust her own assets and the assets in the marital trust, both of which will be subject to tax at her death, before she taps into the assets in the credit shelter trust. Having language establishing the grantor's intent that the marital trust be used first helps where there is an independent trustee. Ordinarily, a trustee must treat current and future beneficiaries equally. A trustee might be inclined to make distributions to the spouse from the credit shelter trust even if she does not need it in order to satisfy the obligation to be fair to all beneficiaries. This language exempts the trustee from making distributions to the spouse when there are other assets available. However, the clause does ensure that first priority for all distributions from the trust will be in favor of the spouse. Thus, if there is not enough available to make distributions to the spouse and other beneficiaries, the spouse will receive distributions before the other beneficiaries. This language also overrides the general rule that the interests of all beneficiaries ordinarily should be given equal consideration.

While it is preferable for the spouse to access the assets of this trust last, it is important to keep this language precatory rather than mandatory. It is possible that the assets in the marital trust may be of a nature that they do not lend themselves easily to providing support for the spouse. If the marital trust held real estate or a family business, it may not have sufficient liquidity to support the spouse. If this clause mandated exhaustion of the marital trust before the credit shelter trust could be tapped, the trustee would be forced to sell the real estate or business to support the spouse. Such a rigid rule likely would be contrary to the best interests of the family.

> 4. ***Withdrawal Power.*** *In addition, the Trustees shall pay from the principal of the trust to my wife, upon written request, an amount that shall not exceed the greater of (i) Five Thousand Dollars ($5,000) or (ii) five percent (5%) of the principal of the trust (valued as of the first business day of the calendar year for which such withdrawal is available). This annual*

> right to request withdrawal may be exercised only during the month of December, it shall be non-cumulative and it shall lapse at the end of such year to the extent it has not been exercised during the year. The power to withdraw principal under this subsection may be exercised only by delivering a written request to the Trustees of this trust that specifically refers to this withdrawal power.

As discussed in the context of an ascertainable standard, the unlimited right to access trust property is a general power of appointment under IRC §2041, and the property subject to the power will be included in the estate of the power-holder. The unilateral right to withdraw trust property is a general power of appointment. If the power to withdraw is not exercised, the failure to exercise will be treated as a gift from the power-holder to the ultimate taker. However, if the unexercised power of withdrawal is a *de minimis* amount, the failure to exercise the power (i.e., the lapse or release of the power) will not be treated as a gift and will not be subject to tax. The Internal Revenue Service does not leave the interpretation of *"de minimis"* open to interpretation. Under IRS Regulation 20.2041-3, the lapse or release of a power to withdraw the greater of $5,000 or 5 percent of the trust value is considered a *de minimis* amount that will not be treated as a gift. This is commonly referred to as a "5 or 5 power." In a credit shelter trust that is funded with $2 million, the withdrawal right would be $100,000 per year. As the trust grows, the withdrawal power also grows.

In light of this generous exception to the rule, the ability to withdraw the greater of $5,000 or 5 percent of the trust value is a popular clause. It guarantees a certain amount to the spouse each year, regardless of the predisposition of the trustee to make or withhold distributions. Where the spouse is the trustee, and there is little likelihood of objection by the descendants, such a clause probably is not necessary. However, if the spouse is not a trustee, if the children and the spouse may fight about distributions, as may happen in a second marriage situation, or if the spouse has some urgent need for guaranteed income, this clause can be appropriate.[47]

The mechanics of the power to withdraw $5,000 or 5 percent is important. This power is limited to the greater of $5,000 or 5 percent per year as required by the regulations. If the spouse does not exercise the power, it is non-cumulative, which means that if she does not exercise it in the given year, it lapses and she cannot exercise the right to the lapsed amount in future years. Of course, in each year a new $5,000 or 5 percent right arises. This clause requires that the determination of 5 percent be based on the value of the trust on a given day. For convenience, the first business day of the calendar year is chosen. It could be based on the last day of the prior year or the first day of any given month or any other date. The key is that there be some specific date to look to in order to determine the value of the trust so the 5 percent value can be determined with specificity.

The power to withdraw under this clause is limited to the month of December in each year. The reason for this limitation is to mitigate the risk of having the greater of $5,000 or 5 percent subject to tax in the estate of the surviving spouse. As indicated, this right to make a withdrawal is a general power of appointment. If the spouse dies on a day when she has the right to make a withdrawal, the amount subject to the withdrawal power will be subject to estate tax in the estate of the surviving spouse. Tax-exempt property would be converted into taxable property. By limiting withdrawal to a single month, the risk is reduced because the tax will only apply if the spouse dies in December. Some practitioners go further and limit withdrawal only to a single day, such as the last day of the year. Some go so far as to exclude the power altogether unless the spouse truly will need to make this withdrawal for the reasons discussed above. These restrictions make sense from a tax perspective. As a practical matter, however, it can be inconvenient to limit the spouse's right of withdrawal in

---

[47] There are two potential tax disadvantages of this clause. Trust income up to $5,000 or 5 percent will be carried out to the spouse even if she does not make the withdrawal. Also, it has been argued that if the spouse does not exercise the withdrawal power, the transferor of the property for GST tax purposes may become the spouse, rather than the grantor. See, however, Regulation 26.2652(a)(5), Ex. 5, which appears to exempt a 5 or 5 power from changing the transferor for GST tax purposes because it is not a gift. Many tax practitioners prefer to avoid use of this clause entirely in the credit shelter trust unless it is essential for the protection of the spouse.

this manner because the dates may not coincide with the timing of actual need of the funds.

It is important to balance the need for withdrawals with the risk of tax liability. If the power amounts to the right to withdraw $100,000, the estate tax liability will be in the range of $50,000 or more if there is also state tax liability. Remember that the trustee still has discretion to make distributions of income and principal in addition to the $5,000 or 5 percent withdrawal power if the spouse needs additional funds. Thus, it is rare that the spouse really would need to exercise the withdrawal power for basic support. As such, the balance should err on the side of no power or a power limited to a short timeframe of a month or a day in order to reduce the estate tax risks.

> 5. ***Termination of Trust.*** *At the death of my wife, the Trustees shall distribute any remaining principal of this trust to or for the benefit of such individuals or charitable organizations, on whatever terms and conditions, including in further trust, as my wife shall appoint by her Will, expressly referring to and exercising this power; provided, however, that this power shall be exercisable only in favor of a descendant of mine, if any descendant of mine is living, and, in any event, shall not be exercisable to any extent for the benefit of my wife, my wife's estate, or the creditors of either. Any such property not effectively appointed by my wife shall be disposed of pursuant to Article VI.*

The credit shelter trust is designed to last for the lifetime of the surviving spouse. Once the spouse dies, it has served its primary purpose of providing for the spouse while avoiding all estate tax at the death of the survivor. If the grantor's primary goal is to give the spouse the maximum degree of control and use of the trust is solely for tax planning and creditor protection purposes, the spouse should be given a power to direct how the property will be distributed at death. This clause grants a power of appointment to the spouse, allowing her to direct distribution in any manner among the descendants of the grantor or charity. If there are no living descendants, she can appoint to anyone. This power can be tailored in a variety of ways to accomplish different goals of the grantor. For example, the power could exclude charity and be limited only to descendants. The clause could be broader to allow distribution to a broader class than just descendants.

The one thing this clause cannot permit is the ability of the spouse to appoint the property to herself, her estate, her creditors, or the creditors of her estate. Under IRC §2041, such a power is a general power of appointment and is subject to estate tax at the death of the power-holder. Since the entire purpose of establishing the credit shelter trust is to avoid tax at the death of the survivor, such a result would defeat the entire purpose of the trust. This clause expressly prohibits exercise in favor of any of those four takers. When those takers are precluded, the power is referred to as a special power of appointment, or a limited power of appointment.[48] Such powers are not subject to estate tax.

Upon the death of the survivor, if the spouse does not exercise her limited power of appointment, the trust still terminates and the property must be directed somewhere. It can either be distributed outright to successor beneficiaries or in further trust. This clause directs the property to be disposed of according to the terms of Article VI. When making reference to another article, it is important to confirm that the proper reference is made. Article VI in the sample trust document is the clause designed to dispose of the trust property at the death of the surviving spouse.

> **(B) Residuary Marital Share.** *If my wife survives me, the Trustees shall hold the balance of the Residuary Trust Estate in a separate trust hereunder (called the "Marital Trust") to be disposed of as follows:*

Section B is the second component of the spousal provisions. Once the credit shelter trust is established and funded, the balance of the trust estate passes to the spouse in order to qualify for the estate tax marital deduction. This clause elects to make the distribution for the spouse in trust. The

---

[48] A special power of appointment, sometimes also called a limited power of appointment, is any power that permits appointment to any person other than the holder of the power, the holder's estate, the creditors of the holder, or the creditors of the holder's estate. A general power of appointment is a power that permits appointment to the holder of the power, the holder's estate, the creditors of the holder, or the creditors of the holder's estate.

clause could make an outright distribution instead. See Appendix B for language to make an outright distribution or an outright distribution with a disclaimer trust.

> **1. Distributions.** *The Trustees shall pay or apply all of the net income thereof to or for the benefit of my wife at least annually. The Trustee also may pay or apply so much or all of the principal thereof as the Trustees consider advisable to provide for the maintenance in health and reasonable comfort, and support in accustomed manner of living of my wife. In addition, the Independent Trustee may distribute so much or all of the principal thereof to my wife as the Independent Trustee considers advisable in its sole, absolute and uncontrolled discretion for any purposes whatsoever.*

The terms of distribution under this clause are significantly different from the terms of the credit shelter trust. For a trust to qualify for the marital deduction, it must meet certain strict requirements set forth in IRC §2056.[49] This clause is creating a QTIP trust under IRC §2056(b)(7). To qualify for the marital deduction, the trust must provide that all income from the trust must be distributed to the spouse at least annually.[50] Many marital trusts call for quarterly distribution of income. This is not required by the Internal Revenue Code, but is merely a practical requirement that distribution of income will be made more than once per year. Monthly income distribution may place an undue burden on the trustee to determine the amount of income and make a timely distribution.

Mandatory quarterly income distributions may be appropriate where there is a risk that the spouse will not receive timely income distributions, as may be the case when she is not the trustee. Such a provision, however, can have adverse implications for tax and creditor protection purposes. In the year of the death of the spouse, if income must be distributed on a quarterly basis, income must be distributed to the estate of the spouse for past quarters. If

---

[49] See the introductory discussion of the estate tax marital deduction regarding additional requirements for non-citizen spouses.

[50] See IRC §2056(b)(7)(B)(ii).

income is distributable only on an annual basis, income need not be distributed to the spouse's estate in the year of death. For example, if the trust requires quarterly income payments, and the spouse dies in April, the income from the first quarter through the end of March must be distributed to the estate of the spouse (unless it was previously distributed). If, by contrast, income is payable yearly, the accumulated income need not be distributed to the spouse's estate. Rather, it can be held in the trust and distributed to the remainder beneficiaries (who may be different from the beneficiaries of the estate of the surviving spouse).

Many older trust forms include a clause that requires income accumulated since the last income payment through the date of death (i.e., stub income) in the marital trust to be distributed to the estate of the spouse, regardless of whether income is payable annually or more frequently. Some current trust documents retain this language. Originally, payment of stub income to the estate was necessary in order to qualify the trust for the marital deduction. However, the stub income need not be distributed to the estate of the surviving spouse. Nonetheless, the value of the stub income will be subject to tax in the estate of the surviving spouse.[51] It is important to consider the relative merits of requiring payment of stub income as well as income payments more frequent than annual in each case. If the beneficiaries of the spouse's estate are likely to be the same as the beneficiaries designated by the grantor, it may not matter. If they are different, it is essential to craft the trust in such a way to minimize the amount that will pass to the estate of the surviving spouse.

Minimizing income payments to the spouse and the spouse's estate also makes sense from the perspective of creditor protection. While the income remains in the trust, it is not subject to the claims of the spouse's creditors. Once the income must be distributed pursuant to the terms of the trust, it is available to satisfy the claims of creditors. If income is distributable annually and stub income is not required to be paid to the estate of the spouse, creditors ordinarily will not be able to access the income in the year of death.

---

[51] See Treasury Regulation §20.2056(b)-7(d)(4) regarding non-payment to the estate, and §20.2044-1(d)(2) regarding the taxation of the stub income in the estate of the surviving spouse.

Another statutory requirement for marital trusts is that the spouse must be the sole beneficiary of the trust. It is not necessary that any principal be distributed to the spouse. The trust could provide that the spouse receives only income. However, no other person may be a beneficiary of the principal (or income) while the spouse is living. This marital trust, as drafted, allows the spouse, as trustee, to make distributions of principal to herself for health, reasonable comfort, and support.[52] In addition, the clause permits an independent trustee to make distributions of principal for any purpose. The distribution of principal could be circumscribed in any manner.

> **2. Withdrawal Power.** *In addition, the Trustees shall pay from the principal of the trust to my wife, upon written request, an amount that shall not exceed the greater of (i) Five Thousand Dollars ($5,000) or (ii) five percent (5%) of the principal of the trust (valued as of the first business day of the calendar year for which such withdrawal is available). This annual right to request withdrawal may be exercised only during the month of December, it shall be noncumulative and it shall lapse at the end of such year to the extent it has not been exercised during the year. The power to withdraw principal under this subsection may be exercised only by delivering a written request to the Trustees of this trust that specifically refers to this withdrawal power.*

This 5 or 5 clause is identical to the withdrawal right set forth in Section A of this article. The principals of this clause apply equally here. It is important to note, however, that the efforts to avoid taxation of the 5 or 5 power under the credit shelter trust are less compelling under the marital trust. Ordinarily the entire marital trust will be included in the estate of the surviving spouse. It is possible to be more flexible with the 5 or 5

---

[52] See the analysis of Section A of Article III for a discussion of the reasons to limit distributions by this ascertainable standard. Although the marital trust typically will be included in the estate of the surviving spouse pursuant to IRC §2044 regardless of whether there is an ascertainable standard, it is still wise to include an ascertainable standard in the event an election to qualify the trust for the marital deduction is not made, as may be the case in de-coupled states.

withdrawal right in the marital trust than in the credit shelter trust. Indeed, it is worth considering inclusion of this clause in the marital trust while excluding it entirely from the credit shelter trust for the reasons discussed in that section. However, it also is worth incorporating the limitations on the 5 or 5 withdrawal power if there is any chance that a QTIP election will not be made and, therefore, the trust otherwise will be exempt from estate tax at the death of the spouse. This is most likely to be relevant in states that are or may be de-coupled.

> 3. *Termination of Trust.* *At the death of my wife, the Trustees shall distribute any remaining principal of this trust to or for the benefit of such individuals or charitable organizations, whatever terms and conditions, including in further trust, as my wife shall appoint by her Will, expressly referring to and exercising this power; provided, however, that this power shall be exercisable only in favor of a descendant of mine, if any descendant of mine is living, and, in any event, shall not be exercisable to any extent for the benefit of my wife, my wife's estate, or the creditors of either. Any such property not effectively appointed by my wife shall be disposed of pursuant to Article VI.*

This termination clause is identical to the termination clause under the credit shelter trust under Section A of this article. The analysis of the clause is the same under this Section B.

> 4. *Qualification for Marital Deduction.* *If my fiduciaries shall elect to qualify part or all of the property passing under this section for the state or federal estate tax marital deduction in my estate, no property shall be allocated to the Marital Trust that does not qualify for such marital deduction and, to the extent possible, no property shall be allocated to the Marital Trust as to which a foreign death tax credit is available. In addition, if my Executor shall elect to qualify part or all of the property passing under this section for the state or federal estate tax marital*

> *deduction in my estate, my spouse may, by written instrument, direct the Trustee to make any property held by the Marital Trust (including any property held in a retirement plan) productive of income within a reasonable time. This right is exclusive to my spouse and may not be exercised by any other person or entity. Whether or not my fiduciaries shall make such election, I intend to take advantage of the state and federal estate tax marital deductions, and all provisions of this Agreement shall be construed and all powers and discretion hereby conferred shall be exercised accordingly, anything in this Agreement to the contrary notwithstanding.*

In addition to the requirement that all income must be distributed to the surviving spouse at least annually, there are several other requirements under IRC §2056 that must be contained within the trust agreement in order to ensure that the trust will qualify as a QTIP trust and thus be eligible for an election that will allow it to qualify for the marital deduction. This clause is designed to incorporate those basic provisions. There are other requirements elsewhere in the trust agreement that relate to trustee powers or other administrative matters that also are incorporated as a result of the marital deduction rules. The application of the marital deduction to those provisions is discussed in the analysis of those clauses.

As previously indicated, simply because a marital trust is eligible for the marital deduction does not mean it automatically qualifies for the marital deduction. It is necessary for the executor of the grantor's estate[53] to elect to qualify the trust for the marital deduction by making a QTIP election on Schedule M of the estate tax return filed for the grantor's estate (Form 706). The additional limitations in this clause are applicable only if an election is actually made. First, there are certain types of property that would not qualify for the marital deduction, such as certain terminating annuities. If these assets are added to the marital trust, the marital deduction will fail. The clause needs to exclude those types of property from being added to

---

[53] If no executor or administrator of the grantor's estate is appointed, the trustee of the revocable trust, as the party in possession of the grantor's assets, can prepare and file the estate tax return.

the marital trust. The trust also excludes any property that would qualify for a foreign death tax credit under IRC §2014. If property is subject to a foreign death tax, the owner is entitled to a credit for the taxes paid. The exclusion of the foreign death tax credit property is intended to allow that property to be excluded from the marital trust, since it is exempt from tax. If the property is excluded from the marital trust, the terms of Subsection 1 of Section A provide that it will instead be added to the credit shelter trust.

A primary motive underlying IRC §2056 is to ensure that the surviving spouse receives all of the income from property that will qualify for the marital deduction. This goal could be undermined by mere allocation of assets held by the trust. If the marital trust is invested in illiquid or growth assets that do not produce income, there would be no income to distribute to the spouse. To protect the spouse, the law requires that the spouse must have the right to require the trustee to make the trust property productive of income.[54] Thus, if the property is invested in non-income-producing real estate, the spouse can order that it be sold and the proceeds invested in income-producing assets. It is essential to limit this right to the spouse, as this clause does. In many cases, the method of investing assets can be used by the trustee, with the consent of the spouse, to prevent the payment of income when doing so would be desirable. For example, if the spouse has creditors who are making claims, the income of the trust is available to satisfy those creditors because the trust requires payment of the income to the spouse. However, if there is no income, there is nothing with which the creditors must be satisfied. If the creditors could exercise the spouse's right to require the property to be made productive of income, that would undermine the trustee's ability to protect the trust property from claims of creditors.

The final sentence of this clause is a savings provision. Since the fundamental rule of trust (or will) interpretation is to ascertain and give effect to the intent of the grantor or testator, this language is designed to express the grantor's intention that the marital deduction be able to apply to

---

[54] The right also must extend to any retirement plan that is held by the marital trust. While a thorough discussion of the rules relating to tax and estate planning with retirement plan assets is beyond the scope of this book, it is important to understand those rules if the grantor owns retirement plan assets. See Natalie Choate's *Life and Death Planning for Retirement Benefits*, sixth edition (Ataxplan Publications, 2006).

the marital trust. There are a variety of unexpected powers that could void the applicability of the marital deduction. Thus, any ambiguity or improper power should be construed in a manner that will allow the trust to qualify for the marital deduction. The intent of the grantor is established at the time of execution. Since the grantor does not know whether his executor will elect to qualify the trust for the marital deduction after his death, it must be clear that the interpretation of the document based on the intent of the grantor must apply regardless of whether the trust is, in fact, qualified for the marital deduction as a result of a QTIP election.

> **5. *Disclaimer.*** *If any portion of the Marital Share is disclaimed by my spouse or by the Trustees, such disclaimed property shall be added to the Credit Shelter Share.*

There are some circumstances where it may be desirable to over-fund the credit shelter trust. For example, if the credit shelter trust is funded only with the maximum state exemption amount and the balance is added to the marital trust, some of the federal exemption may be lost. If the spouse or trustee of the marital trust properly disclaims some portion of the assets that would otherwise pass to the marital trust, those disclaimed assets will be added to the credit shelter trust.[55] The addition of assets to the credit shelter trust would incur a state tax at the death of the first spouse to die. However, the assets in the credit shelter trust will be exempt from both state and federal taxes at the death of the survivor. Since state death taxes are usually considerably lower than federal estate taxes (graduated rates from 5 to 17 percent in most states, as opposed to the federal flat rate of 45 percent), it may be preferable to pay the smaller state tax at the first death and maximize the use of the federal estate tax exemption. Of course, it is preferable to plan to maximize the use of the federal exemption and state exemptions while avoiding state taxes at the first death, as discussed in the introduction to this section. The option of disclaimer should be used only as a last resort in the event that planning fails, and not as a primary planning tool. If disclaimers are intended to be used as a planning tool, there are broader provisions that should be incorporated. See Appendix B for language regarding use of disclaimers as a planning tool.

---

[55] See the analysis of Section O of Article XII for a detailed discussion of disclaimers.

There also may be reasons to incur federal estate taxes at the first death by over-funding the credit shelter trust. An estate is entitled to a credit for prior estate taxes paid if an asset of the estate was subject to estate tax in another estate within the preceding ten years under IRC §2013. In cases where one spouse died within ten years of the other spouse, there was an economic advantage to paying tax in the first estate at lower rates than in the second estate at higher rates, particularly where the second estate received a credit for those taxes paid in the first estate. Prior to the enactment of the Economic Growth and Tax Relief Reconciliation Act in 2001, the estate tax was imposed at a graduated rate. Now that the graduated rate system is on hold, there is less advantage to this planning technique. However, the pre-2001 rates and rules are scheduled to be reinstated in 2011, and this option may once again be a viable post-death planning tool.

> **(C) *Distribution if Grantor Survives.*** *If my wife does not survive me, the Residuary Trust Estate shall be disposed of pursuant to Article VI.*

This Section C disposes of the trust property if the spouse predeceases the grantor. It is important for the trust to incorporate alternate provisions to deal with either contingency. It is possible for the grantor to amend the trust to make disposition if the spouse predeceases, but it is risky to rely on that option. If the couple dies in a common accident or if the grantor is incapacitated at the time of the spouse's death, the option to amend is not available. The full provisions regarding the distribution to children could be set forth in this section. However, since all three sections of this article contain provisions for the ultimate distribution at the death of both spouses, it is more efficient to have each section refer to a separate article that controls the distribution to children.

Article VI

Article VI sets forth the disposition of property at the second death. This clause assumes there are surviving children and that they are the sole beneficiaries of the estate. However, if there are other beneficiaries such as charities, extended family members, or friends, they all can be included as beneficiaries in this article. See Appendix B for some alternative clauses with respect to dispositions at the death of both spouses.

Article VI. *Provisions for Descendants.*

Any property directed to be disposed of pursuant to this Article shall be divided into separate shares, per stirpes, with respect to my then living descendants, and such shares shall be disposed of as follows:

This clause immediately divides all of the property directed to this article among the grantor's descendants, *per stirpes*. This essentially means all living children will receive an equal share, with the share of any deceased child passing to his or her children, or among the surviving children if the deceased child has no descendants.[56]

(A) *Distributions of Trust Property.* The Trustees shall hold the share of each such descendant (hereafter, the "Primary Beneficiary") in a separate trust hereunder. The Trustees may distribute so much or all of the net income and principal of each trust to one or more members of the class of individuals consisting of the Primary Beneficiary and his or her descendants who are living from time to time during the term of the trust, in such shares and proportions, without requirement of equality, as the Trustees consider advisable to provide for the education, maintenance in health and reasonable comfort, and support in accustomed manner of living of any one or more of such individuals. In addition, the Independent Trustee may distribute so much or all of the net income and principal thereof to one or more members of such class, in such shares and proportions, without requirement of equality, as the Independent Trustee considers advisable in its sole, absolute and uncontrolled discretion for any purposes whatsoever. The Trustees shall accumulate and add to principal at least annually any net income not so paid. The Trustees shall give first

---

[56] See the analysis of Section F of Article I for a full discussion of the meaning of the term *"per stirpes."*

> *consideration to the needs of the Primary Beneficiary before making distributions to other eligible beneficiaries.*

The opening sentence of this clause provides that the share determined with respect to each child will be held in a separate trust. The child (or more remote descendant) for whom the trust is determined is identified as the primary beneficiary. This is an important distinction and definition. For all purposes under the trust agreement, the term "Primary Beneficiary," with initial capitalization, indicates a reference only to the descendant for whom the trust under this article was established. Because all of the primary beneficiary's descendants are permitted beneficiaries of the trusts under this article, it is important to differentiate the rights of the primary beneficiary as compared to the rights of other beneficiaries. There are several other clauses where the primary beneficiary has certain powers or rights, and it is essential that there be a term to distinguish the primary beneficiary from other beneficiaries. It is acceptable to use any term for this purpose, so long as it is clearly identified. The use of initial capitalization is helpful to distinguish this as a defined term.

The language of this clause relating to distributions is very similar to the language of the dispositive provisions of the credit shelter trust under Section A.2 of Article V above, except that the primary beneficiary stands in the place of the spouse. The analysis here is essentially the same as there. Under this clause, the primary beneficiary and all of his or her descendants are permitted recipients of discretionary income and principal. There are a substantial number of alternative distribution terms for the children's trusts, a sampling of which would include:

- The primary beneficiary is the only permitted beneficiary.
- The primary beneficiary must receive all of the income at least annually (or quarterly), and the descendants of the primary beneficiary may or may not be permissible principal beneficiaries.
- The primary beneficiary (and possibly the descendants) is entitled to receive only a specified percentage of the trust value each year, such as 4 percent (referred to as a unitrust amount).
- Distributions may be limited to be available only for a specific purpose, such as education or medical needs, or may be broadened

- to include payment for a wedding, purchase of a home, starting a business, and so on.
- Distributions may be permitted only if the beneficiary achieves certain goals such as graduation from college or the receipt of a minimum earned income, referred to generally as incentive trusts.

Incentive trusts have received a great deal of press in recent years and are touted as a way to encourage children to achieve their potential without being "trust fund babies." These trusts are designed to permit distributions only if the beneficiary reaches certain goals, such as graduating from college or earning a certain amount of income per year. While this is a laudable goal, it is essential that an incentive trust be drafted to provide adequate flexibility. The primary problem with incentive trusts is the difficulty in measuring the success of the beneficiary. A beneficiary who joins the Peace Corp or becomes a teacher may not qualify for distributions, thus forcing the beneficiary to make life choices they otherwise may not make. A beneficiary with a catastrophic illness may need distributions for medical care that will be unavailable under the incentive terms. All of these possibilities should be considered and dealt with in drafting an incentive trust. Also, if the original beneficiary fails to meet the requirements of the incentive provisions, an alternate taker should be included. These same considerations also should apply when considering establishing an income-only trust or a unitrust where principal distributions in excess of the unitrust amount are not permitted.

With the variety of options available for the terms of distributions from the trust, it is important for a grantor to consider carefully his goals and objectives before adopting one standard form. It also is important to consider who will act as trustee, as that may be an important component of the decision with respect to the terms of distribution. If the trustee has little or no discretion, as is the case in an all-income, income-only, or unitrust, the choice of trustee only impacts investment and management of the trust fund. Having the beneficiary serve as trustee in such cases may be a better option. If the trustee has discretion over distributions, then having the beneficiary serve as trustee may not be the best option. Note, however, that the clause as drafted would allow the beneficiary to serve as trustee because distributions are limited to an ascertainable standard.

(B) *Primary Beneficiary Withdrawal Rights.* *After attaining each of the following ages, the Primary Beneficiary shall have the cumulative right to withdraw from the trust principal an amount equal to the following fractions of the value of the trust (as well as the following fractions of the value of any subsequent additions to the trust principal, as of the date of the addition): (i) one-third (1/3) after reaching the age of thirty (30) years; (ii) one-half (1/2) after reaching the age of thirty-five (35) years; and (iii) all or any part of the remaining value of the trust after reaching the age of forty (40) years. This right shall be cumulative and shall be exercisable as of the date the Primary Beneficiary attains such age or as of such date as the Primary Beneficiary's trust is funded, if later. The fractions hereunder shall be calculated by reducing such value by any amount which could have been withdrawn earlier but was not. The power to withdraw principal hereunder may be exercised only by delivery of a written instrument to the Trustees of such trust, or by a Will, specifically referring to the withdrawal power.*

Some trusts are designed to last for the lifetime of the primary beneficiary. Other trusts are designed to terminate when the beneficiary reaches a specific age. This clause is designed to make periodic distributions to the beneficiary at three specific ages. As drafted, the clause gives the primary beneficiary the unilateral right to withdraw a specified amount of the trust property in three stages. The number of permutations for this clause, while not unlimited, is certainly substantial. The clause could be limited to a single age, or more than three ages, or it could allow less than full withdrawal. Rather than ages, the clause might reference events, such as graduation from college, marriage, or an anniversary of the grantor's death. If the grantor prefers a lifetime trust, the elimination of this clause would accomplish that goal. If the grantor wants the trust to end, a clause of this nature should be included.

It is possible to alter this clause so that the trustee is obligated to terminate the trust and distribute trust property to the primary beneficiary at stated times, but that provides less flexibility. By allowing the beneficiary to withdraw the property, the beneficiary has the flexibility to decide how to proceed. If the beneficiary does not want to terminate the trust, the beneficiary can elect not to make a withdrawal of trust property and the trust will continue. However, even if the trust continues, any estate tax or creditor protection benefits are lost as soon as the beneficiary reaches the specified age. It is possible to incorporate a power to withdraw the greater of $5,000 or 5 percent into the trust for descendants. The language to do so is substantially the same as in Section A and B of Article V. The 5 or 5 withdrawal power may be in addition to or in lieu of the withdrawal powers under this clause. Alternatively, the grantor may elect to provide for no unilateral withdrawal rights.

An exercise of the right of withdrawal requires a written request that specifically references this power to withdraw. This power to withdraw assets constitutes a general power of appointment and, as discussed in Section P of Article XII, a general power of appointment should not be exercised inadvertently. Calculating the fraction also requires some consideration of various factors. It is possible that the grantor may die after a child reaches one or more of the specified ages and the trust will not be funded at the time a child reaches the stated age.[57] Thus, the beneficiary's right of withdrawal arises on the date they reach the specified age, if the trust is then funded, otherwise it arises immediately when the trust is later funded. Also, since the beneficiary is not required to make a withdrawal, the calculation of the percentage subject to withdrawal must be calculated as if the beneficiary made the prior withdrawal.

> **(C) *Limited Power of Appointment.*** *At the death of the Primary Beneficiary, the Trustees shall distribute any remaining principal of the trust to or for the benefit of such individuals or charitable organizations, on whatever terms and conditions, including in further trust, as the Primary Beneficiary shall appoint by his or her Will, expressly referring to and exercising this power; provided, however, that this power shall be exercisable only in favor of a*

---

[57] Many grantors are concerned that the language of this clause gives the beneficiary automatic access to the grantor's trust property at the specified ages, regardless of whether the grantor is living. Since the trust under Article VI is not created until after the death of the grantor, the terms of this clause are not operative while the grantor is living.

> descendant of mine, if any descendant of mine is living, and, in any event, shall not be exercisable to any extent for the benefit of the Primary Beneficiary, his or her estate, or the creditors of either.

The ability of the primary beneficiary to direct the disposition of trust property remaining at death is substantially similar to the spouse's right to appoint property under Section A and B of Article V. The scope of the power can be as broad or as limited as the grantor desires. As drafted, the clause is relatively restricted, permitting appointment only among the lineal descendants of the grantor. The grantor may wish to permit appointment in favor of charity or in favor of the spouse of the primary beneficiary. An outright distribution to a spouse may result in the property passing outside of the family. One option is to permit appointment in favor of the spouse only in a trust, or allowing the spouse only the income from the property. When contemplating permitting appointment or any other distribution in favor of the spouse of a descendant, it is important to consider the impact of same-gender marriage or civil union laws and the impact those rules may have on the legal definition of a spouse. In this changing area of law, it is important to define whether a spouse for purposes of the trust will include a partner of the same gender.

> **(D)** *Disposition of Remaining Trust Property.* *Any remaining trust principal not effectively appointed by the Primary Beneficiary shall be divided into separate shares, per stirpes, with respect to the then living descendants of the Primary Beneficiary, if any. If the Primary Beneficiary has no descendants then living, such property shall be divided into separate shares, per stirpes, with respect to the then living descendants of the nearest ancestor of the Primary Beneficiary who also is a descendant of mine, if any, or if none, such property shall be divided into separate shares, per stirpes, with respect to my then living descendants. If I have no descendants then living, such property shall be disposed of pursuant to the Article entitled Family Disaster. Any share determined pursuant to this section shall be added to the trust, if any, of which such descendant is a Primary Beneficiary under this Article, or, if none,*

> *shall be held by the Trustees in a separate trust for such descendant pursuant to this Article.*

If the beneficiary fails to exercise the power of appointment granted in the preceding clause, or if there is no power of appointment granted to the beneficiary, this clause controls the disposition of the remaining trust property at the death of the primary beneficiary. Since it is possible that this trust will last through multiple generations, particularly if there is no withdrawal clause included, this clause deals with the possibility that the primary beneficiary may be a grandchild or more remote descendant of the grantor. Initially, the trust property will be divided among the descendants of the primary beneficiary *per stirpes* (as defined in Article I), and the share for each descendant continues in trust on the same terms. If the primary beneficiary has no descendants, the property is distributed among the "descendants of the nearest ancestor of the Primary Beneficiary who also is a descendant of [the grantor]." This essentially means the siblings of the primary beneficiary, and it applies only where the primary beneficiary is a grandchild or more remote descendant of the grantor. If the preceding two clauses are ineffective because there are no living descendants in that line, the property passes *per stirpes* to the descendants of the grantor. In the event there are no living descendants of the grantor, the property is directed to be disposed of according the terms of the "family disaster" clause (see Article VII). If a trust already exists under Article VI for the benefit of a beneficiary who will receive a share under this provision, the share is added to the existing trust. If no trust yet exists, the trustee will create a new trust for that share on the same terms as identified under this article.

Article VII

Article VII.   Family Disaster.

> *If, upon the termination of any trust hereunder, any property is not effectively disposed of by any other provision of this Agreement, or if any property is directed to be disposed of pursuant to this Article, as the case may be, such property shall be distributed to ABC Charity, Inc., for its general, tax-exempt use and purposes.*

It is important to provide for an ultimate taker of trust property in the event all of the potential beneficiaries are deceased. This prospect becomes more probable in situations where the trusts are designed to last for multiple generations. Naming a charity often is the easiest choice, since it is likely that the charity will be in existence for the long term. Also, if the named charity is not then in existence, the trustee can distribute to a different charity with a similar purpose. Charitable organizations can have both charitable and non-charitable purposes. A distribution to charity should always provide that the contribution is to be used for the charity's tax-exempt purposes in order to qualify the bequest for the charitable deduction. The reference to "general purposes" should be used only if the grantor does not intend to apply restrictions to the contributions. If the grantor does wish to place restrictions on the use of the gift, they should be spelled out as clearly as possible.

Most charitable organization have a preference for how bequests are made. They also may have a legal name that differs from their commonly used name. Where a charity has separate, local chapters, it is important to distinguish whether the bequest is made to the national organization or to the local chapter. Before naming a charity as a beneficiary of any bequest under a trust, it is wise to do some online research or contact the charity directly to determine how best to make the bequest. A charity should be willing to share its tax exemption letter from the Internal Revenue Service to prove it is a qualified charity and that the bequest will be eligible for the estate tax charitable deduction under IRC §2055.[58] These general rules regarding charitable bequests should be followed for any charitable bequest, whether or not it is part of the family disaster clause.

If the grantor does not wish to name a charity as the ultimate taker, it is possible to name specific individuals, but in such cases, it is also important to name alternate takers in the event the named takers also are deceased. It also is possible to use a generic class of beneficiaries, such as the "legal heirs" of the grantor. However, it is important that legal heir be a defined term in the document if that type of designation is made.

---

[58] IRS Publication 78, *Cumulative List of Organizations Described in 170(c) of Internal Revenue Code of 1986*, is a list of all organization that have been qualified as a charitable entity for which a deduction will be allowed. The Internal Revenue Service Web site also has a list, which can be found at www.irs.gov/charity/articles.

Article VIII

> **Article VIII.** *Spendthrift Provision.*
>
> *One of my primary purposes in establishing this trust is to protect the trust estate from claims of the beneficiaries' creditors and to protect the assets from the improvidence of any beneficiary. Accordingly, the income and principal of any trust hereunder shall be used only for the personal benefit of the designated beneficiaries of the trust, and no distributions or expenditures of trust assets shall be made except to or for the benefit of such beneficiary. To the maximum extent permitted by law, a beneficiary's interest in the income and principal of this trust shall not be subject to voluntary or involuntary transfer. Without in any way limiting the generality of the foregoing: (i) no beneficiary shall have any right to anticipate, transfer or encumber any part of any interest in the trust estate; (ii) no beneficiary's interest shall be liable for such beneficiary's debts or obligations (including alimony) or be subject to attachment, levy, or other legal process; and (iii) each beneficiary's interest in the trust estate shall constitute the separate property of the beneficiary and shall be free from any right, title, interest, or control of the beneficiary's spouse.*

From the grantor's perspective, the spendthrift clause may be the most important provision in the document. There are two primary motives for creating a trust that will last beyond the lifetime of the grantor. One is to obtain tax benefits, and the other is to gain a degree of protection for the beneficiaries from their creditors or their own lack of prudence in managing their finances. The spendthrift clause is designed to serve the latter purpose by protecting the trust assets from the claims of creditors of the beneficiary and the imprudence of the beneficiary.

Generally, if one individual creates a trust for the benefit of another and further instructs that the beneficiary's interest cannot be transferred to another, the trust will be deemed a spendthrift trust. The assets of a spendthrift trust will be protected against attachment by any creditor in the event the beneficiary is sued or there are claims of liability against the beneficiary.[59] The law is even broader in some states. If the trustee has discretion to retain income and/or provide for the support of the beneficiary, the trust may be treated as a spendthrift trust even in the absence of this express trust language. State law governing the requirements necessary to create a spendthrift trust should be consulted. However, where creditor protection is a goal, express language should be included, regardless of the terms of state law.

The language of this clause sets forth in unambiguous terms that the grantor's primary purpose is to protect the trust as a spendthrift trust from the claims of creditors and from the beneficiary's own improvident decision-making. This spendthrift provision is very broad. It provides that beneficiaries cannot transfer or pledge their interest in the trust to another. It also provides that trust property cannot be used to satisfy any claims against the beneficiary and cannot be attached by creditors.

Another primary objective of parents in establishing trusts for their children is to protect the inheritance of their children in the event of a divorce. Under ordinary circumstances, the trusts established by a parent for the benefit of a child, permitting discretionary distributions by a trustee, would not be subject to division as marital property of the beneficiary in the event of divorce. This spendthrift clause reinforces that general presumption. However, the division of marital property is governed by state law, both statutory and case law. It is important to review local law to determine whether the provision of this spendthrift clause would be sufficient or whether additional distribution limitations are needed.

There is another caveat to the use of spendthrift trusts to provide divorce protection for beneficiaries. Marital property settlements tend to be equitable proceedings. This means the court can divide the marital property based on the court's perception of fairness. Thus, although the trust may not be considered as marital property and therefore not subject to division, the court can modify the division of the marital property to take account of the existence of the trust. For example, if a couple has $1 million of marital property, all things being equal, the court might divide the property equally, giving each spouse $500,000. If the wife is the beneficiary of a trust

---

[59] The Federal Bankruptcy Code provides in Section 541(c)(2) protection for spendthrift trusts by excluding them from the bankruptcy estate.

established by her parents worth $500,000, the court may elect to divide the marital property with 75 percent ($750,000) passing to the husband and 25 percent ($250,000) to the wife. Because the wife has the trust, the court may consider this a fair division of property. Thus, although trusts often are touted as an ideal alternative to pre-nuptial agreements and a good way to protect children in the event of a divorce because the trust itself is not subject to a claim by the divorcing spouse, it may not always have the desired effect.

Another particular concern with respect to spendthrift clauses is that over time, creditors have had some success in pulling down this bastion of protection for spendthrift trusts. Certain super-creditors have been given an opportunity to attach assets of a spendthrift trust where that historically would not have been permitted. For example, courts have attached spendthrift trusts to satisfy an order to the beneficiary to pay child support and, in some cases, alimony. In addition, the states have been successful in attacking trusts for the benefit of elderly or disabled beneficiaries who are receiving public assistance.[60]

These decisions may be understandable from a public policy perspective—individuals who are the beneficiaries of trust funds should not be able to avoid payment of child support or receive public assistance. Unfortunately, they are not legally sound. A spendthrift trust is exempt from creditors because the grantor limited use of the property in that fashion. When viewed in the context that this is the grantor's property that can be used only as prescribed by the grantor, all creditors of a beneficiary are created equal. No particular creditor, regardless of how worthy, deserves an opportunity for recovery that is denied to others similarly situated. These anomalies in the law make bad precedent. Any creditor can argue that if the state or a child can reach the funds, there is no legally defensible argument that another creditor (such as a victim of a car accident or a hospital that provided medical services) should be denied access to the trust funds. This is the classic "first step" down the slippery slope.

---

[60] Section 503 of the Uniform Trust Code incorporates a statutory provision to allow these super-creditors to attach assets in a spendthrift trust. Many commentators have argued that the breadth of Section 503 virtually eviscerates the benefits of spendthrift clauses.

As the use of trusts has become more prevalent, and more creditors have been denied recovery where a trust exists, the courts have been sympathetic to the creditor's claims of unfairness. Occasionally, courts that want to breach a spendthrift trust to provide for creditors fall back on the argument that the grantor did not really intend to create a spendthrift trust. More than one court has asserted that the spendthrift clause is mere "boilerplate" language buried in the back of the document by the drafting lawyer, and the grantor probably never even knew it was there or what it meant. Such judicial arrogance is not surprising when judges tend to come from a litigation background and have little knowledge or experience of the art of drafting. Nonetheless, it is precisely because of this risk that the spendthrift clause is set forth in its own article immediately following the key dispositive terms of the trust. This prominence, along with the unequivocal statement of the grantor's intent, hopefully, will convince a court that the grantor did understand the clause and its objectives.

Article IX

Article IX.   *Termination of Trusts.*

Anything in this Agreement to the contrary notwithstanding, the Independent Trustee is authorized to terminate any trust under this Agreement if the Independent Trustee determines, in its sole, absolute and uncontrolled discretion, that it is not economical or otherwise in the best interests of the beneficiaries of such trust to keep such trust in existence. The decision of the Independent Trustee to terminate or not to terminate any trust hereunder shall be binding and conclusive upon all persons interested in such trust, and, to the extent permitted by law, is not subject to review by any court or administrative tribunal. The determination of whether it is economical to maintain a trust shall be made without regard to any statutory provision with respect to the termination of "small" trusts. In making the determination of whether to terminate any trust hereunder, the Independent Trustee shall give primary consideration to the interests of the current eligible income beneficiaries of such trust. Upon the termination of any trust pursuant to this Article, the Independent Trustee shall distribute any remaining income and principal of such trust to any one or more of the current eligible income beneficiaries of the terminating trust as the

> *Independent Trustee, in its sole, absolute and uncontrolled discretion considers advisable; provided, however, that the Independent Trustee may, in its sole, absolute and uncontrolled discretion, elect to distribute the remaining trust property to a separate trust for the benefit of any one or more of the current eligible income beneficiaries of the terminating trust upon whatever terms and conditions the Independent Trustee deems advisable.*

The "termination of trust" clause is an escape hatch. Modern trust law has evolved significantly over time. As trusts have become more popular as part of the average estate plan, the demand for flexibility in trusts has grown. Where the primary reason to establish a trust is to provide protection from creditors or to gain some tax advantage, grantors may want the beneficiaries to have rights that are as close to outright ownership as possible while still achieving the goals of tax savings and creditor protection. Also, if the burdens of keeping the trust outweigh the benefits, there should be a way to terminate the trust relationship.

Older trusts, even as late as the middle part of the last century, tended to be very rigid and were designed to last for a specified period of time—until the beneficiary reached a certain age or an event occurred, such as marriage of the beneficiary, or even for the longest possible period permitted by law.[61] There was little flexibility in these trusts allowing for the termination of the trust. This lack of flexibility, combined with other terms of the trusts, such as limits on distribution or the need for a corporate trustee, often alienated beneficiaries and left them frustrated with the lack of control over what they perceived as their own money.

This frustration led beneficiaries to seek relief in the courts. The courts of most jurisdictions developed law that all of the trust beneficiaries (and the grantor, if still living) could petition the court to seek termination of the trust. However, under most of these laws, in order to terminate the trust, it would be necessary for the beneficiaries to prove that the trust no longer served a "material purpose" of the grantor.[62] For example, if the trust provides that it is to be used to educate all of the grantor's children, and

---

[61] See the analysis of Section H of Article XII regarding the duration of trusts.

[62] See also Uniform Trust Code §410 et. seq.

some of his children are still minors, a material purpose remains and the trust cannot be terminated. If, by contrast, all of the grantor's children have post-graduate degrees and are well established in their careers, a court may be persuaded that the material purpose of the trust (i.e. education of his children) is met. It is equally possible, however, that a judge could conclude that as long as a child is living, he may require further education, and so a petition to terminate might be denied. Trusts often are not this straightforward, and they often use more ambiguous standards, like "support" of the beneficiary. In such cases, judges are left with the responsibility of determining what the grantor intended, often in the absence of any compelling evidence.

A further obstacle most beneficiaries face in seeking judicial termination of a trust is the existence of a spendthrift clause in the trust. The question arose whether a spendthrift clause designed to protect beneficiaries from creditors constituted a material purpose of the trust. Because courts were inclined to assist beneficiaries who sought to terminate trusts, some courts have reached the absurd conclusion that a spendthrift clause is not a material purpose of the trust. Section 411 of the Uniform Trust Code codifies this rule by holding that a spendthrift clause does not constitute a material purpose of a trust when termination is sought. This rule gave the courts authority to terminate trusts with spendthrift clauses when it otherwise made sense to do so, but it wrecks havoc with the viability of spendthrift clauses.

Between the common law rules and the statutory provisions for the termination of trusts, most beneficiaries now have the right to seek judicial termination of trusts. Unfortunately, the beneficiaries are left to the whims and vagaries of a court. Even if the beneficiaries are successful, they are forced to spend time and money petitioning the court for approval to terminate the trust. The inclusion of this termination of trust clause gives the independent trustee authority to terminate the trust if the independent trustee determines it is in the best interest of the beneficiaries to do so, without the need to obtain court approval.

The terms of the clause are relatively self-explanatory. The language of this clause is designed to give the greatest possible flexibility to the trustee for the termination of trusts and ultimate distribution of trust assets. It is important to note that only an independent trustee has the right to make the decision to terminate the trust. The reason for this is twofold. If a beneficiary-trustee held this power, it would constitute a general power of appointment and would cause the property to be included in the estate of the beneficiary-trustee. Under IRC §2041, the entire value of the trust property would be subject to tax in the estate of the beneficiary-trustee. This would undermine the tax objectives for creating a trust.

The second reason is simply practical. The ability to terminate a trust is extremely powerful. While it is desirable to avoid the time and expense of court interference, the beneficiaries should be required to obtain the consent of some disinterested third party before terminating the trust.

It may be somewhat disconcerting to give the trustee such unilateral authority to fundamentally alter the disposition of trust assets. Depending on who will act as trustee, limiting the power of the trustee might make sense. To do so, the clause could be modified to require that if a trust is terminated, all of the trust property must be distributed outright to the surviving spouse, if living, otherwise to the primary beneficiary. This would reduce the risk of unfair treatment of beneficiaries. However, it also greatly reduces flexibility. If the spouse or primary beneficiary does not need the trust funds and wants the property to be distributed to a descendant, the trustee would not have the flexibility to do so.

The independent trustee under this clause is given absolute authority to terminate the trust if he determines it is in the best interest of the beneficiaries to do so. The decision of the independent trustee is not subject to approval or disapproval of the courts. This limits the beneficiary's ability to challenge the decision of the independent trustee.[63] It is wise to consider the individual circumstances of each family and decide whether the broad power to terminate and restriction on the court's power to review the decision makes sense.

---

[63] As a practical matter, it is a general rule of fiduciary law that no matter how broad a grant of discretion may be, courts will always have the right to review the acts of a fiduciary for an abuse of the discretion given to him. Thus, although this language claims to prevent court intervention, a court can always overrule the acts of a trustee if the court finds that the trustee abused his discretion. It is a high standard to meet, but it does provide some level of protection for the beneficiaries.

Line-by-Line Analysis

Many states have laws that permit termination of a trust if the trust value is so small that it is not practical to retain the trusts. The value set by statute can range from $20,000 to $100,000 or more. However, the independent trustee is not restrained by this statutory limit. Further, the independent trustee is given permission to consider only the interests of the current income beneficiaries of the trust. Ordinarily, a trustee must consider the interests of current and future beneficiaries with impartiality. If the independent trustee were required to consider the interests of future beneficiaries, termination would virtually never be a viable option.

The independent trustee is given discretion to distribute the trust property to any of the income beneficiaries. It is important to limit distribution among income beneficiaries because of the marital trust. As discussed above, the surviving spouse is the sole income beneficiary during her lifetime. If this clause could be interpreted to permit the trustee to terminate the marital trust and distribute property to someone other than the spouse, the marital deduction would not be allowed. It is critical to recognize the potentially fatal impact that seemingly innocuous boilerplate clauses may have on tax provisions.

Also, the independent trustee has discretion to distribute property to another trust rather than outright. If use of a trust continues to be appropriate, but the terms of the existing trust no longer make sense, the independent trustee can terminate the existing trust and add the property to a different trust with preferable terms for the benefit of some or all of the same beneficiaries. For example, if a beneficiary becomes disabled and the terms of an existing trust would prevent the beneficiary from obtaining much-needed government assistance, the independent trustee could terminate the existing trust and add the trust property to another trust with special terms that might enable the beneficiary to qualify for government benefits.

Article X

The existence of a trustee is one of the three fundamental elements of a trust. In general, if the terms of the governing instrument are inadequate to ensure that a trustee is in office, the beneficiaries can petition the court for the approval of appointment of a trustee. The provisions regarding appointment and service of the trustee are therefore designed to avoid the time and expense of petitioning the court for the appointment of a trustee, as well as to provide control initially in the grantor and, to some greater or lesser degree, in the beneficiaries.

Article X. *Trustees Provisions.*

The following provisions shall apply with respect to the appointment and service of the Trustees:

> **(A) *Initial Trustee.*** My spouse and I shall be the initial co-Trustees hereunder. If either my spouse or I is incapacitated, the other may act as sole Trustee. My spouse shall act as a Trustee of any trust of which my spouse is a beneficiary.

The names of the initial trustees are set forth in the opening clause of the trust agreement. Restating the identity of the initial trustees may not be necessary, but it does serve to reduce the chance for confusion. This clause assumes that both the grantor and his spouse will serve as co-trustees. This provides the greatest flexibility in management of trust assets where the trust is funded during the lifetime of the grantor. Either spouse has access to the assets and can manage the money, much like a joint account. If one spouse becomes incapacitated or dies, the other spouse can continue to manage and distribute funds without interruption.

While having both spouses serve as co-trustees is assumed the best option here, it is not the only option, and many skilled estate planning practitioners prefer other options. The initial trustee may be the grantor alone. This obviously is an appropriate choice where the grantor is not married or where the grantor has concerns about placing too much control in the hands of his spouse. Even where the grantor is married, some practitioners prefer that the grantor act as sole trustee as long as he is capable of doing so. This gives the grantor complete control while he is able to act. When the grantor dies or becomes incapacitated, the instrument should name the spouse as successor trustee. There would be a minor delay associated with notifying financial institutions of the new trustee. There also may be problems of demonstrating that the grantor is incapacitated and unable to act. The key question is whether the benefits of singular control by the grantor outweigh the convenience of joint control and the delays and lack of flexibility that can be avoided with initial co-trustees.

Another option is the appointment of an independent third party as the initial trustee. This option makes sense where the grantor lacks the ability or the desire to manage the trust assets during his lifetime. Many older trusts were uniformly drafted with an independent initial trustee. There was a notion that an independent trustee made the trust more legitimate. It is clear in most states that the self-settled trust, where the grantor is both the trustee and the primary beneficiary, is a viable trust. Many states have adopted statutes expressly acknowledging the validity of these trusts. Even in the absence of statutory protection of these trusts, under the common law, a grantor may serve as trustee of a trust for his own benefit where there are other future beneficiaries. See, for example, Uniform Trust Code §401(b) allowing a declaration of trust.

One possible reason for the appointment of an independent initial trustee is the expectation that the independent trustee will provide creditor protection for the grantor. It should be absolutely clear that a revocable living trust is not meant to provide protection from the grantor's creditors. The use of an independent trustee will do nothing to increase the availability of creditor protection. Even in the absence of express language authorizing the trustee to pay for the grantor's debts and expenses, the mere nature of the trust as amendable and revocable would subject the trust to the claims of creditors. If the goal is to achieve a degree of protection from creditors, there are trust options available.[64] However, the revocable living trust will not accomplish this goal and should not be relied upon for that purpose.

> **(B)** *Appointment of Successor Trustees.* My sister, BETTY ROE, is appointed as a Trustee of each trust hereunder, to act together with any other then acting

---

[64] For example, several states, including Alaska and Delaware, allow a grantor to establish a non-revocable trust for his own benefit with an independent trustee and, if certain criteria are met, the trust property will be exempt from claims of creditors. In addition, in some states it is possible to establish a non-revocable trust providing all of the income to the grantor and the property will be exempt from creditor claims. This trust often is used in planning for Medicaid eligibility. However, these trusts are very different from revocable living trusts.

> Trustee, upon the first to occur of: (i) my death [**or:** the death of the survivor of my wife and me], (ii) appointment by me, or (iii) a complete vacancy in the office of Trustee, including by reason of the incapacity of all of the then-acting Trustees. If BETTY ROE fails to qualify or ceases to act as Trustee, her husband, ROBERT ROE, is appointed as a Trustee, to act together with any other then-acting Trustee.

This clause allows for the automatic appointment of a successor trustee. As drafted, the named successor would take office upon the occurrence of any one of three specified events. The first event is the death of the grantor. As drafted, the named successor will act as co-trustee with the spouse. If the spouse is intended to be the sole trustee, the parenthetical alternative naming the successor trustee to act only after the death of both spouses should be adopted. The second event gives the grantor the flexibility to name the successor at any time while he is living, as sole trustee or as a co-trustee, in the event he no longer feels able or willing to continue to act as trustee. The final event names the successor to act if there is no other trustee acting and neither of the preceding options apply to the situation. This might occur if the grantor is deceased and the spouse becomes incapacitated, or vice versa.

It is important to clarify that the successor trustee will act with any other acting trustee in order to avoid confusion. Absent this language, it could be argued that the appointment of a new trustee requires all other acting trustees to cease to act. For example, if the successor trustee comes to office on the death of the grantor, it is important to know that the spouse continues as a co-trustee with the named successor, rather than that the named successor should act alone, effectively removing the spouse as a trustee. The successor trustee clause can list an infinite number of successor trustees. However, if the trust is intended to last for multiple generations, it is likely that at some point there will be no person living who was alive at the time of drafting. The clause at Section D of this article deals with the appointment of further trustees in the event of this contingency.

> **(C) Primary Beneficiary as Trustee.** The Primary Beneficiary of each trust under Article VI, who has

> *attained the age of twenty-one (21) years, is appointed as a Trustee of such trust, to act together with any other then-acting Trustee.*

The children are named to act as trustee (or co-trustee, depending on the provisions of Section B of this article) of their own trusts that are established under Article VI after the death of the grantor and spouse. The trusts under Article VI, though initially for the primary benefit of the children, may continue on for grandchildren and more remote descendants, as each one becomes the primary beneficiary at the passing of the prior generation. This clause therefore names the primary beneficiary rather than the children as trustee. The age limitation is arbitrary. In most states, no one under the age of eighteen could serve as trustee. However, it may be wise to use an older age, such as twenty-five or thirty, to ensure that the primary beneficiary has adequate maturity and experience for the job.

Naming a child as sole trustee of his or her own trust will bring the child closest to outright ownership. It will not, however, protect the trust fund from the unwise decisions of the beneficiary. In some cases, it also may not provide for the maximum creditor protection.[65] An ideal compromise may be to name the primary beneficiary as co-trustee with another trustee. This gives the beneficiary the ability to participate in investment, management, and distribution decisions, but it also protects the beneficiary and the trust property both from waste by the beneficiary and from creditors.

> **(D)** ***Additional and Successor Trustees.*** *After my death or if I am incapacitated, any Trustee then acting is authorized to appoint an additional Trustee or Trustees or a successor Trustee or a succession of successor Trustees to act in the event of any vacancy in his or her office not otherwise provided for above. If, in the event of any vacancy in the office of Trustee, no successor has been named herein or appointed as hereinabove provided, then the following*

---

[65] Some courts have concluded that if the beneficiary is the sole trustee, the trustee can be ordered to make distributions to the creditors of the beneficiary, notwithstanding spendthrift language. While the legal reasoning of these cases may not be particularly sound, the courts are trying to achieve a public policy objective that protects creditors. The merits of such a policy almost certainly depend on the perspective of the parties.

individuals (or groups) who are willing and able to act, in the order listed, may appoint one or more successor Trustees of such trust: (i) my spouse, if living and not then incapacitated; (ii) the Primary Beneficiary of such trust, if any, and if not then incapacitated; (iii) a majority of the other eligible income beneficiaries of such trust who are not then incapacitated; or (iv) a majority of my then-living adult children who are not then incapacitated. If any vacancy in the office of Trustee is not otherwise adequately filled by the foregoing provisions, a court of competent jurisdiction may appoint a successor Trustee. If any Trustee who is or would be an Independent Trustee fails to qualify or ceases to act as a Trustee, and a successor Trustee is appointed pursuant to the terms of this section, such successor Trustee shall qualify only if such successor so named will qualify as an Independent Trustee.

This clause allows any acting trustee to name an additional co-trustee or appoint a successor trustee if there is no other provision for the appointment of a successor. This right only arises if the grantor is deceased or incapacitated, because it is presumed that the grantor will make any change in trustee while he is living and able. If a vacancy does arise and neither the instrument nor the acting trustee appoints a successor, this clause sets a list of options for the appointment of a successor. The spouse has the first right to fill a vacancy if living and capable. This would apply to the credit shelter trust and the marital trust. The primary beneficiary of the Article VI trust for descendants has the next priority. The third and fourth options are designed to deal with appointment under each trust if the spouse or the primary beneficiary is incapacitated. In the credit shelter trust and the descendant's trusts, if the spouse or primary beneficiary, respectively, is incapacitated, a majority of the other capable beneficiaries can fill a vacancy in the office of trustee. With respect to the marital trust, there are no other beneficiaries. Therefore the third option will not work. Rather, the fourth option allows a majority of the adult, capable children to act. If all else fails, a court will have the option to appoint a successor trustee. As noted in the introduction, a trust will fail without a trustee, or the means by which a successor trustee will be appointed. Having the court as a fail-safe to fill a vacancy will avoid that result.

Line-by-Line Analysis

The final sentence of this clause is designed to ensure that regardless of how a successor trustee is appointed under this clause, if the ceasing trustee would have qualified as an independent trustee, the succeeding trustee must also be an independent trustee. The qualifications of an independent trustee are set forth in Section G of Article I. This requirement prevents beneficiaries from appointing themselves or a close relative, such as a spouse, as trustee where the prior trustee was an independent trustee. For example, assume the grantor's daughter is the primary beneficiary of her own trust and is acting as trustee. If she becomes incapacitated and ceases to act as trustee, her spouse could be named as successor trustee because she was not an independent trustee of that trust. However, if as here, the grantor's brother is the ceasing trustee, he would be independent based on the definition set forth in Section G of Article I. As such, another independent trustee would need to be appointed to replace him.

> **(E)** *Removal and Replacement by Grantor. I may at any time and for any reason remove and replace any Trustee, including my spouse, and may name additional or successor Trustees, without regard to any additional or successor Trustee(s) otherwise named herein.*

The grantor has the right to make changes in the office of trustee at any time and for any reason while he is living and capable. Thus, in the event of a divorce, his spouse may cease to act and he can add any co-trustee he prefers. The grantor is not bound by the appointment of a successor trustee already named in the document. If the grantor is alive and capable, but not acting as trustee, he still retains the authority to change the trustee. This broad power should be included in the trust, even if it is otherwise revocable and amendable.

> **(F)** *Removal and Replacement by Spouse. After my death, or if I become incapacitated, then my spouse (if not then incapacitated) shall have the right to remove any Trustee of any trust hereunder and may, but is not obligated to appoint one or more successor Trustees (other than my spouse) without regard to the appointment of any successor otherwise named hereunder; provided, however, that the successor Trustee so appointed would not be a*

related or subordinate party subservient to the wishes of my spouse.

Granting the spouse a broad right to remove and replace a co-trustee is a very substantial power, and it should not be adopted lightly. It is by no means required, and the ramifications should be considered carefully before adopting such a clause. The right should be limited to be effective only after the grantor dies or is incapacitated. Although it may appear obvious that the power to remove could only be done while the spouse is capable, the parenthetical clause also means that an agent acting on behalf of the spouse cannot remove a trustee.[66] This clause also permits the spouse to either decline to appoint a successor to the removed trustee or to appoint a successor trustee without regard to the successor trustee named in the document.

In deciding whether to grant the spouse a power to remove or replace, there are several issues to consider. If the grantor names the spouse as the sole trustee in any event, granting a broad removal power does no harm. Although the spouse is intended to act as sole trustee, other provisions of the agreement allow the spouse to appoint an independent trustee if one is needed to exercise any of the powers that are limited to an independent trustee. Since the spouse can appoint the independent trustee if needed, it makes sense to permit her the option to also remove and replace that trustee. If the spouse will not act as the sole trustee, the reasons for appointing a co-trustee should be considered before granting the spouse the broad power of removal and replacement. If the sole reason to appoint a co-trustee was to aid the level of protection from creditor claims, removal also may be a reasonable option. If a co-trustee (or sole trustee in lieu of the spouse) was appointed because there was some doubt as to the wisdom of the spouse serving as sole trustee, it may not make sense to grant broad removal powers. For example, if the spouse lacks the financial wherewithal to act as sole trustee, it may be appropriate to allow a more limited power of removal and replacement, or none at all. If there is a risk that the spouse and the remainder beneficiaries may be in conflict, as may be the case with a second marriage, having no removal power may be the best option.

---

[66] See the analysis of Section I of this article below for a broader discussion of removal by an agent.

Notwithstanding why a non-spouse trustee is acting, if the trustee is a bank or trust company, it is wise to give the trust beneficiaries the power to remove and replace the trustee. Corporate trustees may be merged with other entities and trust policies, and the trust officers are likely to change over time. The reasons behind the choice of a particular entity as trustee often cease to apply. Also, if the corporate trustee is aware that they cannot be removed except by court action for cause, they may be less attentive to the needs of the beneficiaries. They also may be less willing to work with the beneficiaries on the issue of fees. If there is some compelling need to have a corporate trustee, such as family conflict that requires a completely disinterested party, the replacement power can be limited to appointment of a professional as the successor trustee.

In the absence of a removal clause, courts generally will entertain a petition by the beneficiaries to remove a trustee. Traditionally, the beneficiaries would need to demonstrate good cause for the removal of the trustee. They also may require that all of the beneficiaries, current and future, agree with the removal. Thus, removal can often be accomplished if the beneficiaries are very dissatisfied, but at substantial cost. Professional trustees typically will fight vigorously to avoid a court finding that removal is warranted based on some misconduct. Some, however, often will simply resign in order to avoid such an action. A relatively recent trend has emerged to allow removal of trustees without cause if all the beneficiaries agree. See Uniform Trust Code §706(4). Courts will only grant removal if doing so would not defeat a material purpose of the trust. This gives substantial power to the beneficiaries and may undermine the goals of the grantor in selecting the trustee. It also gives the beneficiaries an opportunity for "trustee shopping" if they do not agree with the decisions of the named trustee. When the choice of trustee was considered by the grantor and is important to achieving the objectives of the trust, it may be worthwhile to incorporate additional language regarding removal. Words to the following effect may be used: "I have selected the individual Trustees after careful consideration and their appointment is material to the purpose of the trust. I have made provisions for the change of Trustees in this agreement as I consider appropriate. No court shall remove a Trustee other than as provided herein, except for good cause shown." This language, while obviously self-serving, should help prevent the use of the no-cause removal statute, and should be employed only where it seems appropriate in light of the family circumstances and the grantor's goals.

This removal clause is drafted very broadly, but it could be more circumscribed. The risk with such a broad clause is that if the spouse does not like the distribution decisions of the existing trustee, she can simply keep changing trustees until she finds one who will do her bidding. If the ability to remove is important, and it typically is in order to preserve maximum flexibility, the replacement power can be limited. In addition to the ability to restrict the spouse's power to replace a removed trustee only with a professional trustee, the spouse's replacement power could be limited to the successor named in the document. The spouse also might be required to obtain the consent of all or a majority of the children in order to remove and replace a trustee. The removal power also could be limited to exercise only once every certain number of years.

Regardless of how the power to remove and replace is modified, the final subordinate clause requiring that the replacement trustee not be "related or subordinate" should always be included in a removal clause. If a beneficiary of a trust has the power to remove a trustee and can replace that trustee with himself or herself, or with a trustee that is subject to control by the beneficiary, the beneficiary is deemed to have all of the powers of the trustee. Since the trustees hold powers that, when held by a beneficiary, would constitute general powers of appointment under IRC §2041, the entire trust would be included under the estate of the beneficiary, even if the beneficiary never exercised that power to remove and replace the trustee with a related or subordinate party.[67]

> **(G) *Removal and Replacement by Primary Beneficiary.*** *The Primary Beneficiary of any trust established under Article VI of this Agreement who has*

---

[67] The key authority on this topic includes the tax court case of *Estate of Wall v. Commissioner*, 101 T.C. 300 (1993), and the government's subsequent pronouncement in Rev. Rul. 95-58, establishing the safe harbor provision that if the power to remove and replace is limited to a trustee who is not related or subordinate, the trust property will not be subject to inclusion in the estate of the holder of the power. The language of Rev. Rul. 95-58 expressly includes the language that the replacement trustee must not be related or subordinate to the beneficiary holding the power to remove and replace, and this language always should be incorporated to attain the safe harbor.

> attained the age of twenty-one (21) years and who is not incapacitated shall have the right to remove any Trustee of such trust and to appoint one or more successor Trustees (other than himself or herself) without regard to the appointment of any successor otherwise named hereunder; provided, however, that the successor Trustee so appointed shall be a professional Trustee who would not be a related or subordinate party subservient to the wishes of the Primary Beneficiary.

The power to remove and replace the trustee can be given to descendants as well as to the spouse. The analysis of the relative merits of granting removal powers to descendants is the same as under the preceding clause. As drafted, this clause defaults to a requirement that the replacement trustee must be a professional trustee. That is not required, but it will serve to limit the risk of trustee shopping by the children, since a professional trustee will be less likely to be persuaded to accede to unreasonable demands by the beneficiaries. The primary beneficiary also must be at least twenty-one years old before exercising the power. This age can be modified as appropriate.

The decision of whether to grant a broad or even a limited removal and replacement power to the children should be based on the same analysis that applied to the decision with respect to the spouse. The ability to replace a corporate trustee also should be a given to children for the same reason. The options for modifying the scope of this clause are similar to those discussed in the preceding clause.

> **(H) *Resignation of Trustee.*** *Any Trustee may resign at any time without the approval of any court by giving written notice of resignation to me, if I am living and not then incapacitated, or to the adult eligible income beneficiaries of the trust, to each co-Trustee, and to each Trustee to be appointed; provided, however, that if no co-Trustee is then acting, such resignation shall become effective only upon the qualification of a successor fiduciary. If a Trustee is incapacitated, such Trustee shall be deemed to have resigned as of the date of the determination of incapacity.*

As surprising as it may seem, trustees generally were not permitted to resign as trustee at the common law. Trustees hold the highest fiduciary duty, and simply abandoning that duty, especially when doing so might have the impact if terminating the trust for lack of a trustee, was simply not permitted. Modern trust law incorporates provisions preserving the trust by allowing for appointment of a successor trustee. However, most states (and the Uniform Trust Code, at §705) still require that the trustee obtain court approval before resigning. This clause allows a trustee to resign at any time without court approval merely by giving written notice. If resignation would create a vacancy in the office of trustee, the resignation will not take effect until a successor is appointed in one of the various ways permitted under the prior clauses. This clause also treats an incapacitated trustee as having resigned, thus allowing for the appointment of a successor, either by the terms of the instrument naming the successor, or one of the several ways identified to fill a vacancy in the office of trustee.

> **(I) Procedure for Resignation, Appointment and Removal.** *The appointment, revocation of appointment or removal of a Trustee shall be made by delivery of a written, signed and acknowledged instrument to the then-acting Trustees and any Trustee to be appointed. Any appointment of a Trustee may be conditioned to commence or cease upon a future event and may be revoked or modified by the individuals or entity entitled to make such appointment at any time prior to the occurrence of such event. Unless otherwise expressly provided, any power to appoint a Trustee shall permit appointment of an individual or a corporation or other entity authorized under the laws of the United States or of any state to administer trusts as Trustee. Any power to appoint, but not a power to remove, a Trustee shall be exercisable by the legal representative of any disabled person holding such power (including the parent acting as natural guardian of any minor beneficiary).*

The process of changing the trustee should not be left to chance or the requirements of state law. The agreement should incorporate provisions for an orderly process to avoid delay, confusion, and the need for court intervention. This clause requires not only that the document of change be in writing, but that the signature be acknowledged before an officer duly authorized to take acknowledgements—ordinarily a notary public, though other officers may be permitted in some states. The requirement of an acknowledgement is intended to prevent fraud, and it is not particularly burdensome when engaging in an act as serious as the change of trustee. However, an acknowledgment is not mandatory, and this requirement could be dispensed with in the agreement.

The appointment of an additional or successor trustee ordinarily would be done in advance of the event that would give rise to the appointment. A trustee authorized to appoint his own successor may prepare a written instrument naming that successor but directing that the appointment will take effect only if the acting trustee dies, resigns, or becomes incapacitated. This clause allows the trustee to make such contingent appointments and allows the trustee to change the appointment prior to it becoming effective by the occurrence of the stated event.

Under the terms of this clause, the power to appoint a trustee can be exercised by a representative of the beneficiary. A representative would include a court-appointed guardian or conservator or an agent acting under a durable power of attorney. Absent the final parenthetical, it would not normally include the parent of a minor beneficiary. Since the power to fill a vacancy in the office of trustee is essential, it is worthwhile to allow a parent to exercise that right on behalf of a minor beneficiary. Not allowing a parent to exercise this power would require the appointment of a court-appointed guardian *ad litem*, or similar fiduciary, to exercise the power. Notably, the power to remove is not extended to a representative. The ability to remove is less critical than the power to appoint and, presumably, only the beneficiary should have that power. If for some reason the power to remove by a representative is desired, it should be expressly stated.

> **(J) Bond.** *No bond or other security shall be required of any Trustee at any time acting for any purpose or in any jurisdiction.*

State law may require that a bond or similar security instrument be posted by a trustee in order to protect the beneficiaries from losses if the trustee engages in mismanagement or malfeasance. The bond, like any insurance policy, requires a premium to be paid, usually on an annual basis. The amount of the bond is dependent on the value of the trust and is paid out of trust principal. This can be relatively expensive protection. Although most trusts incorporate language similar to this clause exempting the trustee from bond, this option should be considered carefully. If the trustee is a bank or trust company, ordinarily there will be sufficient other assets to satisfy the beneficiaries if they successfully sue the trustee for mismanagement or malfeasance. If the trustee is an individual, the ability to recover is far less certain in the absence of a bond if the trustee lacks adequate assets to satisfy the judgment. If the trustee is an attorney or accountant, professional malpractice insurance may provide recovery for mismanagement, but ordinarily would not include coverage for theft of trust property or other intentional malfeasance. The selection of the trustee and the grantor's appetite for insurance typically will inform whether a bond is appropriate. The clause could be modified to exempt bond for the named trustees but require bond of any non-corporate successor trustee.

> **(K)** *Exoneration of Trustee.* *Any individual who is related to me (whether by blood or through marriage) who is serving as a Trustee shall not be liable for any mistake or error of judgment, or for any action taken or omitted, either by the Trustee or by any agent or attorney employed by the Trustee, or for any loss or depreciation in the value of the trust, except in the case of willful misconduct. No Trustee has a duty to examine the transactions of any prior Trustee, and each Trustee is responsible only for those assets that actually are delivered to the Trustee.*

As previously discussed, a trustee is held to the highest standards and will be held personally liable for poor judgment that leads to a loss to the trust. Poor investment choices that result in losses to the trust are the most common basis for personal liability of a trustee. A trustee also may be held liable for improper distribution decisions. For example, if a trustee makes a distribution to a beneficiary based on an ascertainable standard set forth in the agreement and a court concludes that the distribution was outside the bounds of the standard, a trustee ordinarily would be personally liable for that error in judgment. This clause would avoid liability for the improper distribution decisions unless the distribution was made despite the trustee's actual knowledge that it was improper.

Most individuals, especially those who are not professional money managers, would not accept the liability of a trustee. This clause is designed to exempt certain trustees from liability except in the case of willful misconduct. This language protects the limited class of trustees from acts of negligence and even some intentional acts. Liability will be found only where the trustee willfully acted against the interests of the trust, such as in the case of theft or misappropriation of trust assets. The protected trustees in this clause are limited only to individual trustees who are related to the grantor. Corporate trustees are not protected because, as professional money managers receiving a substantial fee for their advice, they should be held liable if their poor decisions result in losses to the trust. The class could be broadened to include any individual trustee.[68] This would incorporate professional trustees, such as attorneys or accountants, and may or may not be desirable. If the grantor is appointing a non-professional individual as trustee who is not related to the grantor, this clause may be broadened to incorporate the named trustee.[69]

Each successor trustee should be excused from examining the conduct of the prior trustees. Ordinarily, a successor trustee would be obligated to review the acts of a prior trustee and to take remedial action to either correct problems or sue the prior trustee if there was some misconduct. Successor trustees do not want this level of liability. Most professional trustees would not agree to appointment as successor if they could be liable for the acts of a prior trustee. Although a non-professional might unwittingly accept appointment subject to such liability, it would be unfair to impose such a risk.

---

[68] The adoption of the Uniform Principal and Income Act in many states protects trustees from liability if they properly select and delegate investment authority to a professional investment advisor. See the analysis of Section O of Article XII for a fuller discussion of this law.

[69] An attorney drafting a trust where the attorney is named as a trustee should be very careful in the use of this clause. Exempting the draftsman from liability ordinarily would constitute a conflict of interest for the attorney with respect to the grantor-client and would require knowing, written waivers. Moreover, some state courts have held that a clause exempting the drafting attorney who serves as trustee from liability would be void. Thus the drafting attorney would be held liable despite this language.

Article XI

Trustees have relatively limited powers at common law. In the absence of express powers written into the trust agreement, the trustees would be required to obtain court approval for most of their actions. For example, trustees do not have an inherent power to buy and sell assets. This would significantly undermine the primary benefits of establishing a revocable trust, which is the avoidance of court interference. Many actions that trustees ordinarily would take that are identified in this "trustee powers" clause, such as acting as an officer of a company owned (in whole or in part) by the trust, or making loans to the trust, would be prohibited acts of self-dealing. It is necessary to include an express authorization for these acts if they are desired.

Some states have adopted a drafting shortcut by establishing a statutory list of trustee powers that could be incorporated into a trust agreement. The statute identifies most of the powers a trustee may need and provides the scope of the exercise of those powers. However, the mere existence of the statute ordinarily is not sufficient. The terms of the statute, or the statute itself, must be referenced in the trust agreement for the statutory powers to apply.

In the days before word processing, the ability to reference a statutory provision in lieu of writing out three or four pages worth of trustee powers was certainly attractive. Now, where trusts can be thirty or forty pages long, it is tempting to use the statutory shortcut to shorten the length of the trust agreement. The pros and cons of relying on the statutory provisions can be debated. In addition to being brief, the statutory powers tend to represent the collective wisdom of the legislature (which typically is informed by trust professionals) regarding the appropriate powers and their scope.[70] However, these assumptions do not work for all grantors at all times. Also, laws change over time. When a trust may last for 100 years or more, a reference to a changed statute may cause confusion. Setting forth the powers fully in the trust can avoid those problems. Nonetheless, the statutory provisions are a good starting point when considering what

---

[70] The Uniform Trust Code sets forth general and specific powers for trustees in Sections 815 and 816. A review of those sections may also provide a helpful starting point in considering what powers should be incorporated into a trust agreement.

powers to provide to the trustee. They should be reviewed in each jurisdiction, and an analysis of the relative merits of each power should be made.

This trustee powers clause is merely one sample of most of the powers that may be incorporated into the trust agreement. The language is simplified and brief to give a flavor of what the clause should do. A review of the grantor's intent and state statutory provisions should be undertaken before incorporating these or any other trustee powers into a trust agreement. Standard trustee powers clauses in most form books incorporate other powers beyond those listed here. Many of those powers, such as the power to delegate or the power to retain an investment advisor, are found elsewhere in the sample trust agreement because they require broad articulation that cannot be readily accomplished in this clause. Most of the powers are self-explanatory and do not require further explanation. Those that do require some additional explanation are discussed in the form of footnotes.

Article XI. *Trustee Powers.*

Without limiting any other powers granted by this Agreement or authorized by law, the Trustees shall have the following powers and discretions, which shall extend to all principal and income held hereunder in any capacity or for any purpose (including accumulated income) until the final and outright distribution thereof, and which the Trustees may exercise with sole, absolute and uncontrolled discretion, without application to or approval by any court:

> **(A)** *To retain, acquire or sell any variety of real or personal property (including any discretionary common trust fund of any corporate fiduciary acting under this document, mutual funds, covered or uncovered stock options, insurance policies on my life and investments in foreign securities), without regard to diversification and without being limited to the investments authorized for trust funds;*[71]

---

[71] Historically, some statutes imposed a limit on the type of assets that could be held in trusts. This paternalistic legislation was intended to protect trust beneficiaries, but it also limited the return on trust investments because the investment options were very

(B) *To enter into agreements for the sale, merger, reorganization, dissolution or consolidation of any property, including corporation or other business entity;*

(C) *To manage, improve, repair, sell, mortgage, lease (including the power to lease for oil and gas), pledge, convey, option or exchange any property and take back purchase money mortgages thereon;*

(D) *To open, close, maintain, draw checks on or otherwise withdraw funds from, and make deposits into bank accounts of any kind;*

(E) *To maintain custody or brokerage accounts (including margin accounts) and to register securities in the name of a nominee;*

(F) *To exercise stock options;*

(G) *To vote and give proxies to vote shares of stock, interest in a partnership, membership interest in a limited liability company or any similar business interest;*

(H) *To make joint investments in any property, whether real or personal; to enter into and act as a general or limited partner in general or limited partnerships; to establish corporations (including limited liability companies) of any kind; and to transfer assets to any such joint ventures, partnerships or corporations;*

---

conservative. This clause allows the trustee to invest broadly and permits the trustee to disregard the requirement of diversification. Even with this broad authorization, courts are quick to hold trustees liable for losses as a result of a failure to diversify or for acquiring or keeping risky asset. Most trustees are unwilling to take that risk. Thus, if the grantor has a particular asset, such as a family home, a closely held business, or other asset that he desires the trustee to retain, it is important to expressly instruct the trustee to retain the property, by name if possible, despite the risk of loss associated with retaining the property.

Line-by-Line Analysis   121

(I) *To serve as an officer or director of any business entity owned, in whole or in part, by any trust hereunder;*

(J) *To compromise and settle all claims by or against any trust or trust property hereunder (including those relating to taxes);*

(K) *To borrow funds from any person or entity (including a Trustee hereunder) and to pledge or mortgage trust assets to secure such loans;*[72]

(L) *To extend, renew or renegotiate loans or guarantees;*

(M) *To lend money to or for the benefit of any person beneficially interested hereunder (including a Guardian);*[73]

(N) *To divide any trust hereunder into separate trusts based on the fair market value of the trust assets at the time of the division;*

(O) *To administer multiple trusts established under this document* in solido;[74] *and*

---

[72] Allowing the trust to borrow from the trustee is an act of self-dealing. The trustee, especially a corporate trustee, may be the best option for borrowing, but it also may place the trustee in a position of conflict with the trust and the beneficiaries. The benefits and risks of including this power should be considered before it is adopted.

[73] The ability to make loans to a beneficiary is a useful power. Some trusts include broader powers that allow trustees to make loans to any person or entity. This can be useful if the trust owns an interest in a closely held business so the trustee can loan trust funds to the entity. The clause could be broadened to permit the trustee to make loans to himself, which ordinarily would be prohibited self-dealing if not expressly authorized and would need to be considered very carefully.

[74] This provision means that if there are multiple trusts, the trustee can co-mingle the assets of the multiple trusts and hold them all in a single account. This may be administratively convenient, but it can lead to problems among beneficiaries if there is a need for unequal distributions or a desire for separate investment strategies. While the power is typically given to trustees, it may not be wise for the trustee to exercise that power.

(P) *To exercise in good faith and with reasonable care all other investment and administrative powers and discretions of an absolute owner that lawfully may be conferred upon a fiduciary.*[75]

Article XII

The administrative clauses of the trust agreement are often pejoratively referred to as the boilerplate. Unfortunately, many practitioners and judges view these as standardized provisions that appear in every trust and, as such, they are not entitled to significant weight if there is some ambiguity or uncertainty regarding the grantor's intent. The administrative provisions establish the framework in which the trust must operate. As indicated, establishment of a trust creates a separate legal entity, much like a corporation. The trust has no guidance for how to operate outside the terms of its governing instrument. The trustee does not know its responsibility and the beneficiaries do not know their rights but for the trust agreement. Where the trust agreement is silent, both the common law and state statutes will fill the gaps and provide a framework. However, as has been seen before, the gap-filling provisions established by law often are not consistent with what the grantor would want, given the option to choose. The "administrative provisions" clause gives the grantor that option. Notwithstanding any provisions of the law, these clauses set forth the grantor's intentions with respect to the process of administering the trust.

Many of the clauses here may be viewed as savings clauses. Many, but certainly not all of the clauses, are designed to provide either estate or income tax protection. They are in some cases redundant of other clauses or are designed to provide a general protective provision in the event that some other clause fails to provide adequate protection. That being the case, it is true that the administrative provisions do appear in all trust agreements (at least those that are well drafted), and there often is little variation among the terms. Nonetheless, each clause has a particular meaning and effect that can be varied. The applicability of each clause should be considered in every case.

---

[75] This final provision is designed to capture any other power a trustee may require that is not expressly stated in the trust instrument. It gives the trustee very broad powers and should be considered carefully before it is granted.

Line-by-Line Analysis

Article XII. *Administrative Provisions.*

The following additional provisions shall apply to all trusts created hereunder:

> **(A) Presumption of Survival.** *No successor beneficiary shall be deemed to have survived the event creating a present interest hereunder in the successor beneficiary unless such beneficiary survives such event by more than thirty (30) days. Notwithstanding the foregoing, my spouse shall be deemed to have survived me if my spouse survives me for any period of time or if the order of our deaths cannot be determined.*

The presumption of survival is intended to prevent the creation of an interest in favor of a beneficiary when the beneficiary dies very soon after his or her predecessor in the trust. This provision is incorporated for administrative efficiency to prevent the opening and immediate closing of a new trust account, or for the need to pay assets to a beneficiary's estate where it will be subject to unnecessary administrative costs and delays. Rather, the interest passes pursuant to the terms of the trust to the next successor beneficiary. Many practitioners incorporate a more robust requirement for survival by establishing a longer period of survival of sixty or ninety days. A thirty-day period is usually adequate to protect against individuals who die in a common accident. Any time period will be arbitrary, and a longer period is fine. However, a period of more than ninety days would seem unduly punitive.[76]

A special exception is carved out with respect to the grantor's spouse. Under this clause, the grantor's spouse is presumed to survive in all circumstances unless there is proof that the spouse died before the grantor. If the spouses are presumed to survive under the trust instrument of each grantor, jointly owned property will be treated as belonging one-half to each spouse. This presumption also allows each grantor to take advantage of the unified credit and marital deductions that are available under federal tax law and most state tax laws. In cases where the ownership of assets is

---

[76] For the marital deduction under federal law to apply, the required period of survival cannot exceed six months. See IRC 2056 §(b)(3).

disproportionate between spouses and one spouse does not have sufficient assets to take full advantage of the unified credit amount, the less wealthy spouse should be the spouse that is presumed to survive. This will allow for the creation of the marital trust in the estate of the wealthier spouse, which in turn enables the estate of the less wealthy spouse to take full advantage of that spouse's unified credit amount.

Under ordinary circumstances, it is best to ensure that when the combined wealth of a couple exceeds twice the unified credit amount, each spouse should own assets equal to the unified credit amount in order to take advantage of the unified credit at death. In some cases, the balancing of wealth is not possible. In those cases, the presumption of survival clause will need to be evaluated to determine which spouse should be presumed to survive. The grantor's trust and the spouses trust would then have different clauses regarding survival.

> **(B)** *Anti-lapse Provision. If any disposition under this Agreement is contingent upon the survival of a beneficiary and the beneficiary does not satisfy the condition of survival, and if there is no substitute taker designated who satisfies the conditions for taking, such disposition shall lapse. The provisions of any anti-lapse statute in any jurisdiction shall not apply to preserve any disposition to or for the benefit of any individual who is not identified as a substitute taker hereunder.*

Virtually all states have a statutory provision that is designed to prevent the lapse of a bequest in a will. These anti-lapse laws generally provide that where a bequest is made to an individual and the will does not provide for an alternate distribution if the individual predeceases the testator, the anti-lapse law will prevent the bequest from lapsing and requires that the bequest pass to the descendants of the deceased beneficiary. These anti-lapse laws are not unlimited. Typically, they are only applicable to bequests to individuals who are closely related to the testator, such as a spouse, child, parent, or sibling of the testator. For example, assume the will provides "I give $10,000 to my brother, Joe Doe." If there is no additional provision, and if the brother predeceases the testator, the anti-lapse laws would provide that the $10,000 bequest would pass to Joe's descendants. If Joe was a distant cousin or friend, the anti-lapse law typically would not save the bequest. The bequest would simply lapse.

It is rarely wise to rely on the terms of a statute to ensure that the testator's desires are carried out. If the testator wants the bequest to pass on to children, or if he prefers that it lapse on his brother's death, that intent should be clearly set forth in the will. In most jurisdictions,, language to the effect that "I give $10,000 to my brother, Joe Doe, if he survives me" is sufficient to defeat the application of any anti-lapse laws. However, in a distinct minority of jurisdictions, even that language is not sufficient to defeat the anti-lapse laws. Additional language, including a statement similar to this "survival and anti-lapse" clause, are necessary to prevent the application of the anti-lapse laws that would preserve this bequest and pass it on to the descendants of the deceased brother. [77]

Anti-lapse laws arose in and are applicable primarily to wills. At least in theory, they have no application to revocable trust unless there is a state law expressly extending the rule to trusts. Unfortunately, because of the nature of the revocable trust as a will substitute, some states have extended this rule by statute, and courts may incorporate this rule into trust law even in the absence of statutory authority. Because of the increasing trend toward treating revocable trusts as will substitutes, it is prudent to incorporate a clause, such as this, directing that any anti-lapse laws will not apply to the trust in order to preserve a bequest to the descendants of a deceased beneficiary unless the trust agreement expressly provides for passing to the descendants.

> **(C)** *Additional Provisions for Payment of Income and Principal. The following provisions shall apply with respect to the payment of income or principal from each trust hereunder:*
>
> > **1.** *Income payments shall be paid at least annually unless accumulation of income is authorized, or some shorter period is expressly provided.*

---

[77] See the analysis of Section B of Article IV for a more detailed discussion of anti-lapse provisions.

2. *Unless otherwise expressly provided, upon the occurrence of any event causing termination of any trust, any accrued and collected, but undistributed income shall be added to principal.*

3. *The Trustees may, without the approval of any court, make distributions of income and principal in cash or in kind, or partly in each, and, may, in their discretion, allocate particular assets or portions thereof to any one or more beneficiaries, without any duty to distribute any asset pro rata among beneficiaries. The Trustees may do so without regard to the income tax basis of specific property allocated to any beneficiary, provided that such property shall be valued for purposes of distribution at its value on the date of distribution.*

4. *Whenever provision is made for distribution of principal or income to any person, the same may instead be applied for the benefit of such person. Application of principal or income for the benefit of a person under any legal disability may be made by payment to or application for the use of such person directly, or in the discretion of the Trustees by payment to such person's parent, spouse, custodian under any gifts or transfers to minors act, guardian, committee or conservator, in whatever jurisdiction appointed, or any one with whom such person resides, and the receipt of the one to whom any such distribution is made shall be a full discharge from accountability to such person. The decision of the Trustees as to the purpose, time and amount of any payment of income or principal shall be binding and conclusive upon all beneficiaries of this Agreement.*

5. *Notwithstanding any other provision of this Agreement or applicable law to the contrary, after my death, or if I am incapacitated, any Trustee who is not*

Line-by-Line Analysis

> an Independent Trustee shall not participate in any discretionary decision unless the discretionary decision is limited by an ascertainable standard as defined in section 2041(b) of the Code and the Regulations thereunder. As used herein, a "discretionary decision" includes any decision regarding the distribution, payment, application, accumulation, or allocation of income or principal, or the termination of a trust.
>
> 6. In making any discretionary decision concerning the distribution of trust property the Trustees may (but shall not be required to) take into consideration other resources reasonably available to the beneficiary eligible to receive the distribution.

There are several portions of the trust agreement where distributions of trust income and principal are contemplated. This clause is designed to apply to all of those provisions without having to reiterate these provisions in multiple places. The first section merely provides that any income must be distributed annually unless some shorter period is provided or accumulation is authorized. The trustee can make more frequent distributions, but this protects the beneficiary by ensuring that distributions will be made at least annually.[78]

Section 2 will ensure that any accumulated income passes to remainder beneficiaries rather than to the estate of the income beneficiary. Originally, for a trust to qualify for the marital deduction under federal law, the trust must include a provision that all accumulated but undistributed income must be paid to the estate of the spouse after the death of the spouse. The Internal Revenue Service eliminated that rule, and now payment to the spouse's estate is no longer required.

Avoiding payment of trust income to the estate of an income beneficiary can be very beneficial. Accumulated but undistributed income can be fairly substantial. If that income is distributed to the estate of the income

---

[78] This clause also will ensure that the marital trust qualifies for the marital deduction, which requires that all income be paid at least annually, if that trust provision inadvertently fails to require annual distribution of income.

beneficiary, it is subject to any claims against the estate, and it will be distributed to the beneficiaries of the estate. The beneficiaries of the estate may not be the same as the successor trust beneficiaries. For example, a grantor may create a trust for the benefit of his child and, upon the death of the child, for the child's children. The grantor may not make any provisions for the child's spouse, having no intention of benefiting the spouse. If the accumulated income is paid to the child's estate, the spouse may well be the sole beneficiary of the estate and will receive all of the income. If instead the income is accumulated and added to trust principal, the property will pass on to the grantor's grandchildren, as intended.

Section 3 is designed to give the trustee broad discretion in making distributions of trust property to trust beneficiaries. A clause of this nature is helpful to the trustee because it makes distribution decisions easier. Allowing an in-kind distribution rather than forcing the liquidation of assets in order to make a distribution will avoid capital gains or losses on the sale of assets just to accomplish a distribution when there is no other compelling reason to sell the property. Absent a clause of this nature, or some law to the contrary, trustees would be required to divide property proportionately among beneficiaries. For example, if the trust requires one-half of the trust property to be distributed to each of two beneficiaries, the trustee would be required to distribute one-half of every trust asset to each beneficiary. This can be very impractical and could be detrimental to the financial interests of the beneficiaries. This clause allows the trustee to allocate different assets to each beneficiary so long as the fair market value of the total distributed assets is the same.

In addition to the practical benefits of this clause, there are compelling underlying tax reasons to include this language. Where a fractional share marital funding clause is used, as discussed in the analysis of Section A of Article V, a clause of this nature is essential. Dividing the marital share and the credit share on a fractional basis would be overly burdensome and unworkable if each share had to receive a proportionate share of every asset. Also, the ability to choose highly appreciating assets for the credit trust and income-producing assets for the marital trust are important elements of post-mortem tax planning. Without this language, those options would not be available to the trustee.

The clause also excuses the trustee from considering the tax basis of the property in making the distribution of trust property. Tax basis is the value associated with property for the purpose of determining capital gains or losses. Usually, basis is determined based on the original cost to acquire the property, plus the cost of any improvements. When the property is later sold, the sale price, less the basis, equals the capital gain (or loss, as the case may be). The capital gains tax is imposed on the amount of that gain. Thus, basis is very important in considering the "real" value of property. If the trustee distributes two assets to separate beneficiaries, each with a fair market value of $100, but the basis of one asset is $5 and the basis of the other asset is $95, the distribution really is not equal. The low-basis asset will require the beneficiary to pay significantly more tax when the asset is sold, reducing the net value of his share significantly as compared to the beneficiary who received the high-basis asset.

Ordinarily, when a trustee makes a distribution of trust property, it is appropriate to consider the tax basis in the property. The final sentence thus seems counterintuitive in that it allows the trustee the discretion not to consider basis when the property is distributed based on its fair market value at date of distribution. Not surprisingly, this clause is included for income tax planning purposes. It is necessary to avoid the realization of gain when a "pick-and-choose fractional funding formula" is used, as is the case in this sample trust. For a detailed discussion of the seven different marital deduction funding clauses, as well as the relevance of income tax basis, see Sebastian V. Grassi Jr.'s *A Practical Guide to Drafting Marital Deduction Trusts* (ALI-ABA, 2004), Chapter 15.

The provisions of Section 4 protect the trustee by allowing distributions to be made for the benefit of a beneficiary rather than directly to the beneficiary. This is particularly helpful where the beneficiary is somehow incapacitated, either because the beneficiary is a minor, has a cognitive deficiency, or otherwise is not prepared to make financial decisions. By allowing distributions to a responsible party and protecting the trustee from claims by the beneficiary, this clause enables the trustee to act in the best interest of the beneficiary without fear of reprisal. Although the concluding sentence is designed to prevent any judicial review of the trustee's decisions, courts of equity in virtually all jurisdictions have the right to review a trustee's decisions for an abuse of discretion. Thus the beneficiary is protected if there is actual malfeasance by the trustee.

The fifth section of the clause is designed to protect a beneficiary-trustee from tax liability. The analysis of Section A of Article III contains a detailed discussion of the need for an ascertainable standard and the potential tax liability of a beneficiary-trustee. This clause is a blanket prohibition against any non-independent trustee exercising any power that would cause the trust assets to be included in the estate of the trustee. This savings clause is designed to protect a beneficiary-trustee if the other trust language incorporating ascertainable standards or limiting certain acts to the independent trustee is inadvertently excluded. Use of a savings clause such as this is wise, because even the most careful draftsman may inadvertently fail to incorporate a necessary protection, and the tax liability for such a mistake can be extraordinary.

The final clause should be reviewed carefully, and the impact considered before it is incorporated. When a trust provides that distributions may be made to a beneficiary for a specific purpose, such as health, education, or support, the question arises whether the trustee should make distributions regardless of whether the beneficiary has other resources with which to meet those needs. The primary question is whether the trust is truly intended to be treated as if it is an asset of the primary beneficiary or whether the future beneficiaries are a significant consideration. When the trust is created merely for tax purposes or creditor protection and, in the absence of those considerations, the grantor would have given the property outright to the beneficiary, it makes sense to employ a clause, like this one, where the trustee should not care whether the beneficiary really needs the requested distribution. If, by contrast, the goal of the trust is to create a fund that is available to meet the needs of the primary beneficiary, but for which the grantor hopes to create a multi-generational fund, the clause should be modified to require that the trustee consider whether the beneficiary really needs the distribution based on the beneficiary's other resources.

It is worth noting that corporate trustees, and many other professional trustees, will typically require that the beneficiary disclose his or her other resources before a discretionary distribution will be made, regardless of the terms of this clause. At a minimum, this typically means the beneficiaries must provide a copy of their annual income tax returns to the trustee. Beneficiaries often find this to be intrusive. Unfortunately, trustees are obligated to consider the interests of current and future beneficiaries and to treat them both fairly. While this clause is designed to excuse them from considering other resource, it is rare that a corporate trustee would do so. This is yet another reason to consider carefully who will serve as the trustee.

> **(D)** *Provisions for Retirement Assets in a Marital Trust. If any trust of which my spouse is the sole income beneficiary is named as the beneficiary of a qualified retirement plan, the Trustees of such trust shall withdraw during the calendar year from the qualified retirement plan an amount equal to the greatest of: (i) the minimum required distribution for the calendar year; (ii) the income generated or deemed to be generated by the assets in the retirement plan for the year; and (iii) the portion of the retirement plan that is treated as trust income for such year under the state law applicable to the administration of such trusts. The Trustee shall distribute to my spouse, as income, an amount that is no less than the greater of (i) the income generated or deemed to be generated by the assets in the retirement plan for the year, or (ii) the portion of the retirement plan that is treated as trust income for such year under the state law applicable to the administration of such trust. No expenses chargeable to principal under applicable state law shall be charged against the income earned by the qualified retirement plan and withdrawn by the Trustees.*

There are advantages to naming the spouse as direct owner of a retirement account, because the spouse can roll over the account into her own name. This will allow the spouse to delay taking minimum distributions until she reaches age seventy and a half and she can take withdrawals over her life expectancy. This delay allows the account to continue to grow tax-free and delays payment of the income tax on withdrawals. In some cases, however, it is necessary to add retirement assets to either the credit shelter trust or the marital trust. This might occur where the account participant has concerns regarding the spouse's ability to manage the assets, where there is a risk of a second marriage, or where the participant wants to ensure control over the distribution of the assets after the death of the spouse, as may occur when there are children of a prior marriage. When it is possible that retirement assets could be added to the marital trust, there are several additional provisions that need to be included to qualify the retirement account assets for the marital deduction. The Uniform Principal and Income Act incorporates provisions regarding the determination of income in a retirement account for state law purposes. This deemed income may be greater than or less than the actual income. Even states that have not adopted the act in full may have laws governing the determination of income in retirement accounts for trust purposes.

In light of the requirement under IRC §2056 that all income generated by the marital trust assets must be distributed to the surviving spouse, this clause requires the trustee to take all of the income (whether actual income or deemed income pursuant to state law rules relating to trust income), regardless of whether that is greater than the amount of the minimum distribution required for the year from the plan, and distribute it to the spouse. The act also includes instructions with respect to whether expenses are to be charged against income, principal, or partially to each. The clause prohibits the trustee from artificially reducing the amount of net income in the retirement account by charging expenses that are properly chargeable against principal against the income.

> **(E)** ***Additions to and Combination of Trusts.*** *If, upon the termination of any trust, any property is set aside in respect of a person for whom another trust is then held hereunder, then such property shall instead be added to the principal of such other trust and administered and disposed of as an integral part thereof. The Independent Trustees may, in their sole, absolute and uncontrolled discretion, combine any trust under this Agreement with any other substantially identical trust established by either or both of my spouse and me.*

In many cases, when a trust terminates, the property will pass outright to an individual who is the beneficiary of another trust under the same agreement. In such cases, this clause will allow the property to be added to the existing trust rather than making an outright distribution to the beneficiary or distribution to a separate trust for that beneficiary. In addition, if the grantor and his spouse each create separate trusts for their children, there may be multiple trusts with similar terms for the same beneficiaries. It can be more costly and administratively inefficient to have multiple trusts. This clause allows those trusts to be combined if they have substantially the same terms.

> **(F) *Governing Law and Situs.*** *The validity, construction and administration of this Agreement and any trust hereunder shall be governed by the laws of Anystate. The Trustees, at any time and for any reason, may transfer the place of administration and assets of any trust to any jurisdiction. It is my expectation and intention that no court approval will be required for such a transfer. However, the Trustees may seek court approval of such transfer if necessary, and I expect the court to approve the transfer as such is consistent with my intent. The Independent Trustees may change the governing law to any jurisdiction at any time and for any reason, provided that a change in the place of administration shall not result in a change in the governing law unless specifically directed by the Independent Trustees. The Independent Trustees may make technical amendments to this Agreement to make any transferred trust valid and effective under the laws of the transferee jurisdiction.*

Ordinarily a trust will be governed by the law of the jurisdiction where the grantor resided at the time the trust was created, or when it became irrevocable (typically at the death of the grantor). However, there may be times when it is preferable to apply the law of a different jurisdiction. Historically, the grantor could not arbitrarily select any jurisdiction just because he prefers the laws of another jurisdiction. In most common law jurisdictions, there must be some significant contacts between the trust and the jurisdiction chosen. The contacts may include the residence of the trustee, the residence of some or all of the beneficiaries, or the location of the trust property.[79] If the grantor elects to apply the law of a state other than the grantor's state of residence, it is preferable to set forth the reasons in the trust agreement. Language similar to the following at the start of the clause ordinarily would be sufficient: "I am a resident of State Nostate, but my Trustee is a resident of State Anystate. Therefore..." However, the Uniform Trust Code, at Section 107, does allow the grantor to arbitrarily select the governing jurisdiction. In states that adopted the Uniform Trust Code, setting forth the reason for the selection would not be necessary.

Giving the independent trustee authority to transfer the trust to another state is helpful. If the trustee resides outside the original jurisdiction, having the trust governed by the law of that other jurisdiction can be costly and burdensome, because it will require legal advice with respect to the law in a jurisdiction with which the trustee is not familiar. This power to change jurisdiction should not be permitted in a beneficiary-trustee, because arguably the beneficiary could transfer the trust to a jurisdiction where the laws are more liberal in favor of beneficiaries. There could be adverse tax consequences to the beneficiary merely because he has the power, even if the beneficiary never exercises the power.

In many cases, when the trustee is a corporate trustee, the principal office of the corporate trustee may be outside the jurisdiction cited in the agreement. In such cases, the trust property may be administered and managed outside the governing jurisdiction. This clause makes clear that the mere fact that the trust property is managed outside of the governing jurisdiction is not enough, by itself, to change the governing law to which the trust is subject.

> **(G)** *Legal Obligations. The trust estate hereunder shall remain available to satisfy any of my legal obligations during my lifetime. Except with respect to the foregoing, no provision of this Agreement shall be construed as relieving any person of his or her legal obligations, including the obligation to support any beneficiary hereunder. No part of the income or principal of any trust hereunder and no*

---

[79] See, for example, Section 403 of the Uniform Trust Code regarding the valid creation of a trust.

> *exercise of a power of appointment granted herein shall be used to satisfy any such legal obligations.*

As discussed elsewhere, the revocable living trust is not designed to protect the trust assets from the claims of the grantor's creditors. Indeed, because the trust is meant to be funded with all of the grantor's assets during his lifetime, it is important that the trust instrument be clear that the trust property can be used by or on behalf of the grantor to pay his debts and obligations. While this provision is important to protect the grantor, the ability of any other trustee to use trust property to satisfy any of his or her personal obligations would have a detrimental tax effect. Under the *Upjohn* case,[80] if a trustee has the ability to use trust assets to satisfy his or her legal obligations, the entire trust property would be subject to estate tax in the estate of the trustee when the trustee dies. For example, if the grantor's child is a beneficiary and trustee of the trust, and the child, as trustee, has the ability to make distributions for the support of the minor children of the child, such a power would permit the beneficiary-trustee to use trust assets to meet her legal obligation to support her minor children. This savings clause is designed to prevent these adverse tax consequences.

> **(H) *Rule against Perpetuities.*** *Each trust hereunder shall terminate upon the expiration of twenty-one (21) years following the death of the survivor of me, my spouse and those of my descendants who are living on the date of my death. At the expiration of such perpetuities vesting period, the Trustees shall pay any remaining income and principal of such trust to the Primary Beneficiary, or, if none, to the then living descendants, per stirpes, of the Primary Beneficiary, or, if none, to my then living descendants, per stirpes, who are eligible income beneficiaries of the trust.*

The rule against perpetuities is perhaps the most arcane and archaic rule in the law. The rule, stemming form the earliest days of trust law, has been stated as follows: an interest in property must vest, if at all, within twenty-one years of the death of the last survivor of the lives in being on the

---

[80] *Upjohn v. United States*, 72-2 U.S. Tax Cas. (CCH) ¶ 12,888 at 86,077-86,078 (W.D. Mich. 1972).

creation of the interest or the interest is void. Many a law student has decided to study medicine after being asked to understand and apply that rule. The underlying premise of the rule is to prevent control by the "dead hand." The law presumed that one person should not be able to control property in perpetuity long after he is dead and gone. At some point, the new "owners" should have control over the property.

Trusts, by their nature, may have perpetual existence. When one trustee dies, a new one automatically succeeds into the office of trustee and ownership of the trust estate continues in the trust. To prevent grantors from creating perpetual trusts, the rule against perpetuities was adopted in the common law. If a grantor created a trust without any end, the law invalidated the trust from the beginning. This was a powerful incentive to force grantors to impose some termination provision. The law does not permit just any termination provision. Rather, the trust must terminate no later than a specific date. That date is determined by looking at all of the beneficiaries who were alive on the date the beneficial interests were created. In the case of a revocable trust, the interest in the beneficiaries is not created until the grantor's death. Thus, as a starting point, the rule looks to all of the potential trust beneficiaries who were alive when the grantor died. Since the trust is for the benefit of spouse and descendants only, the timing and class of "lives in being" is easily determined. The trust must terminate and the property must pass outright no later than twenty-one years after the death of the last beneficiary (the spouse or a descendant of the grantor) who was living when the grantor died. This clause will ensure that regardless of any other provisions in the trust, the trust will be terminated within the maximum perpetuities period permitted by law.

Out of an abundance of caution, some practitioners require termination after twenty years rather than twenty-one years, just to be safe. Some states have modified the common law rule to provide an alternate perpetuities period of a flat ninety-nine years from creation, regardless of lives in being. Yet other states have elected to do away with the rule against perpetuities altogether, or to establish such a long period that they effectively have eliminated the effect of the rule.[81] The goal of eliminating the rule is to

---

[81] For example, Delaware has eliminated the rule entirely, and Florida has a 360-year period.

allow grantors to establish so-called dynasty trusts that can pass through multiple generations without any tax liability at each generation.[82] It is important to review the governing rule in each jurisdiction to determine what language is necessary in this clause to avoid the trust being void from inception for a violation of the rule.

It may be tempting to eliminate this clause when the governing trust provisions provide that the trust will terminate when the children reach a certain age on the assumption that the twenty-one year rule automatically will be met. However, the rule deals with possibilities, not reality. For example, no matter how old the grantor, he or she is presumed to be capable of having more children. If there is any possibility, no matter how remote, that the rule could be violate, the trust is void from the start. This clause will protect against any interpretation that could result in a violation of the rule, no matter how remote.

> **(I)** *Outright Distributions to Minors. If, upon the termination of any trust, any property vests absolutely and free of trust in a minor, and is not otherwise directed to be retained in further trust for such minor under any other provision of this Agreement, then the Trustees may distribute the same to any custodian for such minor under any gifts or transfers to minors act. The Trustees may designate as custodian any person, including any one of the Trustees, who is qualified to act in such capacity. In the alternative, the Trustees may retain and manage the same during the beneficiary's minority, without bond and with all powers and discretion granted to the Trustees by this Agreement or by law. The Trustees may pay or apply the income and principal of such trust for the health, education, support or maintenance of such minor, accumulating any income not so applied, until such minor reaches the age of majority (pursuant to the laws of the jurisdiction where the beneficiary is domiciled) or until the prior death of such minor. At such time, any remaining principal and*

---

[82] To effectively pass through multiple generations without tax, the trust also must be exempt from the GST tax, which is discussed in greater detail in the comments to the introduction to Article V.

> *accumulated income shall be paid to such minor or to his or her estate.*

Ideally, the dispositive trust provisions will incorporate specific language that requires any property passing to minor beneficiaries to be held in trust until the beneficiary reaches an appropriate age. This will allow the grantor to control the management of the property through the trustee and the terms of the trust. However, if there is a requirement that the trust property would otherwise pass outright to a minor, this clause will prevent the need to have a court-appointed guardian of the minor's estate. Most states permit property that otherwise would vest in a minor to be held by a custodian under a Uniform Transfers (or Gifts) to Minors Act. The act provides that the grantor can name a custodian or direct the creation of a custodial account to hold assets passing to a minor. Without this specific direction in the trust, however, it would be necessary to petition the court for approval to transfer to a custodian. In the absence of a custodian under the act, the alternative is to seek appointment of a guardian of the estate by a court. Appointment as guardian of the estate typically requires continuing judicial oversight. The guardian must account to the court. While this can provide protection against misuse of the funds, it also can be expensive and time-consuming. Many states permit a parent of a minor child to accept a *de minimis* amount on behalf of a child without being appointed as guardian or custodian, but this option would be available only for relatively small amounts.

This clause gives the trustees the option to elect to hold the property in trust rather than in a custodial relationship. The terms of the custodial relationship are set forth in the act. The terms of a trust are set in this clause. Although the trust may be more flexible, the age of majority in most states is eighteen. By contrast, the age of termination for most custodial accounts is age twenty-one. It is possible to modify the terms of this clause to provide that the trust will last until age twenty-one, rather than the age of majority, if that is preferred. Of course, if sufficient thought is given to this issue to modify this clause, the dispositive provisions regarding distribution should be addressed to avoid the need to rely on this savings clause.

> **(J)** ***Tax Elections.*** *The Trustees and/or the Executor of my estate, in their sole discretion and without the order or*

> *approval of any court, are authorized to make or not make any election, allocation or other discretionary decision permitted under the provisions of any tax law in effect from time to time. My fiduciaries also may make or decline to make equitable adjustments of the interests of the beneficiaries in light of such decisions. Notwithstanding the foregoing grant of discretion, my fiduciaries shall make any adjustment necessary to avoid reducing any marital deduction under any tax law. The Trustees may, except with respect to any trust under this document in which my spouse is the sole income beneficiary, allocate property (or the right to receive property) which is subject to estate tax and federal income tax as income in respect of a decedent to principal, to income, or in part to each. No beneficiary shall have any rights against any fiduciary by reason of any such decisions or adjustments.*

Even in the absence of the first two sentences of this clause, fiduciaries arguably have not only the ability, but the obligation, to make appropriate tax elections to maximize tax savings opportunities. This clause, through the final sentence, merely protects the fiduciary from claims by one beneficiary for maximizing the benefits of another. The more important provisions of this clause are the third and fourth sentences. This clause primarily is designed to protect the qualification of the marital trust for the marital deduction under federal tax law. First, the trustees are obligated to make any elections to avoid reducing the amount of the marital deduction. To qualify for the marital deduction, the trustee cannot be permitted to reduce the amount qualifying for the deduction, such as through the payment of debts or expenses out of the marital deduction property.

The fourth sentence deals with a unique type of property interest known as "income in respect of a decedent." This is property that is subject to both estate tax at death and income tax, and it is governed by Section 691 of the Internal Revenue Code. The most common form of this property is retirement assets. This clause gives the trustee broad authority to treat such property as either income or principal, or both. However, to protect the marital deduction, the trustee is prohibited from doing so with respect to such property that qualifies for the marital deduction. As discussed above, the allocation of income in respect of a decedent to principal might violate the requirement that all income must be paid to the spouse.

> **(K) Trust Accountings.** *While the trust holds asset worth less than one hundred dollars ($100), the Trustee shall make no accounting. The Trustees may, in their sole discretion, settle any account at any time by agreement or judicially. Any agreement made with those beneficiaries under no legal disability who at the time are currently entitled to the income or presumptively entitled to the principal shall bind all individuals, whether or not then in being or of legal capacity, then or thereafter entitled to the income or principal, and shall release and discharge the Trustees for the acts and proceedings embraced in the account as effectively as a judicial settlement, notwithstanding the circumstance that any Trustee may also be a party to such agreement in a separate capacity, either individually or as a fiduciary of another estate or trust. The Trustees may provide to me, or my guardian or conservator if I am incapacitated, or, after my death, to each eligible income beneficiary and presumptive remainderman (or the parent or legal representative of any such individual who is a minor or is incapacitated), statements of trust transactions at such time and in such form as the Trustees consider advisable. If all such individuals either give written approval of the statement or fail to notify the Trustees in writing of any objection within thirty (30) days of the mailing of the statement to such individuals, the statement shall be final, binding and conclusive on all individuals interested in the trust, regardless of whether such statements would qualify as an accounting pursuant to local law.*

Perhaps the most fundamental duty of a trustee is the duty to account. Because the trustee holds property for the benefit of another, it has long been held to be essential that the trustee advise the beneficiaries on a periodic basis with respect to the property. Most states have statutes governing accountings, or at least local customs regarding the scope of an accounting. At a minimum, an accounting should set forth the nature and

Line-by-Line Analysis 141

value of the assets in the hands of the trustee, a statement of income receipts and expenditures, as well as a summary of changes in the assets. By either law or custom, an accounting also will reflect both the initial book value of assets as well as the current fair market value, and will report any gains or losses on sale of assets.[83]

Depending on the size and nature of the trust assets, an accounting can be very difficult to prepare. They can be expensive as well, if the trustee requires professional assistance in the preparation of the account. The costs of preparing the accounting are borne by the trust, not by the trustee personally. A primary benefit of the accounting, however, is that if the court approves the accounting, after giving the beneficiaries the opportunity to be heard, the trustee will be exempt from liability for any action (or inaction) that was subject to the accounting.

This clause is designed to alleviate some of the burdens on the trustee and save the expense of formal, court-approved accountings, while providing liability protections for the trustee. As noted in the preface to the sample trust agreement, many revocable trusts may not be funded initially, except with a token amount. Absent the opening sentence of this clause, the law would require the trustee to make some accounting. The trustee also is permitted to settle an accounting with the beneficiaries by agreement rather than seek judicial approval. In addition, the accounting can be settled by the current beneficiaries who are adults and capable of understanding the accounting. If they approve the accounting, contingent beneficiaries cannot later complain. Absent this provision, it would be necessary for the courts to appoint a guardian *ad litem* to represent the interests of unborn or unascertained beneficiaries.[84] This would necessitate that all accountings be court-approved.

---

[83] The Uniform Trust Code, at Section 813, provides broad parameters for the duty of the trustee to provide notice to the beneficiaries and to account to the beneficiaries. Under Section 105, certain of these obligations cannot be overridden by the trust agreement. The trustee must be required to provide basic trust information to adult beneficiaries. It is important to review the limits of state law regarding the trustee's duty to account before adopting any clause with respect to the trustee's obligations and rights in that regard.

[84] Some states have adopted laws that allow for virtual representation of beneficiaries in court proceedings without the appointment of a guardian *ad litem*. If there are adult, capable beneficiaries who have substantially the same interest as minor, disabled, unborn, or unascertained beneficiaries, the court can dispense with the appointment of a guardian

The most compelling part of this clause is in the final two sentences. This provision will allow the trustee to provide periodic statements, such as a copy of a trust account investment statement from the account broker, in lieu of a full-blown accounting. While the information provided in account statements is not sufficient to qualify as a full accounting, this will provide the beneficiary with basic account information that is sufficient to give the beneficiary notice of how the account is being managed. It also will alert the beneficiary to purchases and sales in the account, as well as distributions or changes in value. The beneficiary must raise objections and concerns regarding the statement in a timely manner (here, thirty days) or be barred from raising complaints in the future. It may be preferable to provide a longer period, such as ninety days or six months, to allow the beneficiary to observe whether a trend in the statements appears.

A clause of this nature ideally will encourage the trustee to provide more information to the beneficiaries in the hope of obtaining the desired exemption from liability. Full and frequent information is the beneficiary's best defense against an incompetent or malicious trustee. If the beneficiary is forced to wait for an annual or even less frequent court-approved accounting, or to wait until he somehow learns of a possible problem with the account, it may well be too late for the court to intervene on behalf of the beneficiary. Certainly, it will be an expensive and time-consuming endeavor for the beneficiary to protect his rights through the process of court-supervised accountings. On balance, any provision that will encourage the trustee to provide open access to information to the beneficiary is to be encouraged, unless there are extraordinary circumstances and the grantor has some compelling reason to keep information regarding the trust secret.[85]

This clause is very liberal and provides the maximum degree of protection for the trustee. While it does serve to save costs, it does require that the beneficiaries be vigilant of their own interests because they may lose the right to object. Before adopting such a liberal clause, it is important to

---

ad litem. Not all states have adopted this form of legislation and, where it has, it generally only applies to court actions with respect to trusts, not agreed settlements among the trustee and beneficiaries.

[85] Under the Uniform Trust Code, "secret" trusts are not permitted because disclosure to the beneficiaries is a non-waivable obligation of the trustee.

consider who will serve as trustee and the capabilities of the beneficiaries to be diligent in protecting their own interests. As a practical matter, regardless of the broad exemption used in the trust agreement, if the beneficiaries believe that a full, court-supervised accounting is necessary, they can petition the court to require one. Also, if the trustee engages in fraud or abuse, there are many remedies available to protect the beneficiaries against the trustee's breach of duty, regardless of whether a modified accounting is deemed to have been approved under this clause.

(L) *Generation-Skipping Transfer Tax Provisions.*

   1. *The Trustees and/or my Executor may allocate any portion of any federal generation-skipping transfer tax exemption to any property as to which I am the transferor, including any property transferred by me prior to my death. The Independent Trustees also may divide any trust into two separate trusts based on the fair market value of the trust assets at the time of the division, so that the federal generation-skipping transfer tax inclusion ratio for each such trust shall be either zero or one. Such division shall be based on the fair market value of the trust assets at the time of division. The Independent Trustees may allocate additions to any trust so that all trusts or property with an inclusion ratio of zero are allocated to a trust hereunder with an inclusion ratio of zero and all trusts or property with an inclusion ratio of one are allocated to a trust hereunder with an inclusion ratio of one.*

   2. *Any reference to federal generation-skipping transfer tax exemption shall mean the exemption provided for by section 2631 of the Code that has not been allocated by me, by my fiduciaries or by operation of law to property transferred by me during my lifetime or allocated by my fiduciaries to property passing by reason of my death, whether outside this Agreement or under any Article of this Agreement that precedes the disposition of the Residuary Trust Estate.*

3. The term "inclusion ratio" shall have the same meaning as provided in section 2642 of the Code. As used herein, I intend that any reference to a trust having an inclusion ratio of zero shall mean that the trust is exempt from the generation-skipping transfer tax, and any trust that has an inclusion ratio greater than zero shall mean a trust that is subject to generation-skipping transfer tax, in whole or in part.

4. At the death of the Primary Beneficiary of a trust established under this Agreement, if any trust property would pass to or in trust for the descendants of the Primary Beneficiary, then the Primary Beneficiary shall have a general power of appointment limited to the following terms. Such power shall be a power to appoint to the Primary Beneficiary's estate by a Will expressly referring to and exercising such power, the smallest fractional share of such trust property that would reduce to a minimum the aggregate estate, inheritance, succession and generation-skipping transfer taxes payable by reason of the Primary Beneficiary's death. Such fractional share shall be determined as if any power of appointment of the Primary Beneficiary (under this provision or otherwise) is not exercised and the trust principal and the Primary Beneficiary's entire gross estate for federal estate tax purposes are to be distributed to the Primary Beneficiary's descendants.

A number of full legal treatises have been written about planning with respect to the GST tax. The sample trust is *not* designed to maximize the benefits of planning for the use of the GST tax. There are additional terms that should be added to the trust if the goal is to create a dynasty trust that will pass tax-free through multiple generations.[86] Nonetheless, every trust

---

[86] If planning for dynasty trusts that will take advantage of the GST tax exemptions is a goal, there are treatises available on the topic, including, Richard B. Stephens, et. al., *Federal Estate and Gift Taxation*, eighth edition (Warren, Gorham & Lamont of RIA,

Line-by-Line Analysis 145

runs the risk of running afoul of the GST tax rules and creating a GST tax liability. This savings clause is designed to provide flexibility to the trustee to mitigate the tax liability if the GST tax does or may apply.

Section 1 of the clause is a broad grant of discretion to the fiduciaries of the grantor to allocate his available GST exemption in any manner they deem appropriate, including to transfers that were made by the grantor during his lifetime. The reference to the executor is necessary because these elections are made on either gift tax returns (Form 709) or estate tax returns (Form 706), both of which would be prepared by the executor if one is appointed. Under Section 2, the grantor's available GST exemption is defined by reference to the appropriate code section and backing out any exemption that was previously used during life or by pre-residuary bequests. The amount of exemption that remains is available for allocation by the fiduciaries under Section 1.

The trustee also is permitted to divide any trust so that each trust will be fully exempt or fully subject to GST tax. To understand the benefits of this option requires a basic understanding of how the GST tax works with respect to trusts. A trust may be either exempt from GST tax, usually because the available exemption was allocated against the full value of the trust, or it is fully subject to tax because no exemption was allocated to the trust. Either of these trusts is easy to deal with. Whenever a taxable distribution is made from a fully non-exempt trust, the full distribution is subject to GST tax. If a distribution is made from a fully exempt trust, there is no tax liability. The problem arises with a hybrid trust where the available GST exemption was less than the value of the trust and so the trust is partially exempt. If the trust is partially exempt, every distribution is partially taxable subject to a formula, which can be complicated to apply. To avoid this complication, the trustee is given broad authority to divide any trust into two separate trusts based on the appropriate fraction so that one trust will be fully exempt and the other will be fully taxable, thus avoiding the complicating factor of a partially exempt trust.[87]

2002). A thorough understanding of the GST tax rules is essential when actively seeking to maximize the advantages of the GST tax exemption.

[87] The ability to divide trusts based on fair market value is also included in the general trustee powers clause with somewhat less precision than is included in this clause. In a

The clause accomplishes this division by reference to the technical terms used in the code for defining exempt and non-exempt trusts. As provided in Section 3 of the clause, a trust with an inclusion ratio of zero is a fully exempt trust. A trust with an inclusion ratio of one is a fully taxable trust. If the inclusion ratio is between zero and one (i.e., greater than zero), the trust is partially taxable and partially exempt. The trustee is broadly authorized to divide the trusts so each trust has an inclusion ratio of either one or zero, with none in between. To be effective, the regulations require that the division be made based on the fair market value of the trust on the date of division. It cannot be made based on some earlier date when the value may have been lower, thus providing the opportunity to place additional assets in the exempt trust.

The final paragraph of this clause is designed to minimize GST tax liability by requiring the primary beneficiary to pay an estate tax if it would be lower than the GST tax. The clause accomplishes this by creating a general power of appointment (i.e., by allowing the primary beneficiary to appoint a portion of the trust property to his or her own estate).[88] The amount subject to the general power of appointment is a formula expressed as the smallest fractional share of the trust that will minimize all death taxes at the death of the primary beneficiary. For the fraction to work, it must be based on the assumption that the power is not exercised and that the entire trust principal and gross estate pass to descendants. Take the following example. The estate tax exemption is $2 million, the trust is worth $1,000,000, and the primary beneficiary's estate is worth $2 million and passes entirely to the spouse of the primary beneficiary. If the formula did not assume that the entire estate passes to descendants, the primary beneficiary would have no power of appointment because the formula would find that he has a $3 million estate (estate plus trust) and $2 million passes to his spouse, so $1 million is less then his available exemption of $2 million. There would be no right to exercise the power of appointment, and a 45 percent GST tax would be imposed on the trust property. By assuming that the entire estate

---

trust agreement that failed to include this GST savings clause, the general trustee powers clause could be used to accomplish the same ends.

[88] As discussed elsewhere, a beneficiary's ability to appoint property to himself, his estate, or the creditors of either is a general power of appointment, and the property subject to the power will be taxable in the estate of the holder of the power under IRC §2041.

passes to descendants, the formula works to create a combined estate of $3 million, $2 million of which uses the available exemption by passing to descendants and $1 million of which would be subject to estate tax. The question then is whether the estate tax rate is lower than the GST tax. If so, the primary beneficiary will have a general power of appointment over the trust property in order to minimize the GST tax. If the rates are the same and there is no tax benefit to paying a lower estate tax, the primary beneficiary will have no general power of appointment.

Prior to the 2001 transfer tax change that adopted a flat rate of 45 percent for both estate and GST tax transfers, there was a significant benefit to paying the estate tax, at a potentially lower rate, rather than paying the GST tax at the highest possible rate. Now that the GST tax and the estate tax are imposed at the same rate regardless of value, there is less benefit to opting to pay the estate tax rather than the GST tax. However, the tax changes of the Economic Growth and Tax Relief Reconciliation Act are designed to expire on December 31, 2010. Thereafter, the old graduated rate system for the estate tax with a maximum rate applied to GST transfers will be restored. The benefits of paying an estate tax rather than the GST tax would once again apply.[89] As such, it makes sense to continue to include language creating a general power of appointment as a protective measure until such time as the equal flat rates are made permanent. The risk, of course, is that the primary beneficiary is given unrestricted control over the distribution of some portion of the trust property. The grantor may not trust the primary beneficiary with such a broad power. The grantor will need to evaluate the relative risks of unlimited control by the beneficiary against the tax rewards of granting a limited general power in this context.

> **(M)** *Disclaimers.* *Any person (or his or her attorney-in-fact or legal representative, including the executor, administrator, conservator or other personal representative of his or her estate) may irrevocably disclaim, renounce or release any interest, benefit, right, privilege or power granted to such person or entity under this Agreement, in whole or*

---

[89] It is very likely that Congress will act in some fashion prior to 2011 to change the re-institution of the pre-2001 transfer tax laws. If so, the change likely will affect the relative merits of opting to pay either the estate tax or the GST tax, and will inform the merits of a clause similar to this Subsection 4.

in part, without approval of any court. Further, with regard to any interest in property passing to any trust under this Agreement (including a beneficial interest in a trust) or any fiduciary power under this Agreement, the Trustees may irrevocably disclaim, renounce or release any such interest, benefit, right, privilege or power, in whole or in part, without the approval of any court. Any such disclaimer, renunciation or release shall be in writing, signed by the disclaimant, renouncer or releaser in the presence of two disinterested witnesses and shall be duly acknowledged before a proper official for taking acknowledgments and shall comply with any other applicable requirements of local, state and federal law regarding the formalities of execution and delivery of such instruments.

No person is obligated to accept a gratuitous transfer of property. However, if a person is given an interest in property, then declines to accept that property and it passes on to another, that refusal to accept the property typically would result in a gift by the declining donee in favor of the successor donee.[90] Federal gift tax laws permit a donee to decline acceptance of a gratuitous transfer without any gift tax consequences under very limited circumstances by executing a qualified disclaimer. To be a qualified disclaimer, the declination must meet all of the criteria set forth in IRC §2518. It also must comply with any state law requirements for a disclaimer. The two primary requirements to be a qualified disclaimer are that it be in writing and that it be done within nine months from the date the interest was created. Typically, with a disclaimer under a revocable trust, the nine-month time period begins to run on the grantor's date of death. If the disclaimer does not meet the criteria set forth in IRC §2518, the declination to accept the property will still be effective. However, there will be gift tax consequences to that declination.

Disclaimers can be very useful for post-mortem tax planning. Where family circumstances or tax laws change between the time of drafting and the time of death, it may be necessary to adjust the disposition of certain property.

---

[90] Gift tax implications arise only where the property declined by the first donee passes to another donee. If the property would pass back to the donor because of the refusal to accept the property, there are no gift tax concerns.

Line-by-Line Analysis

This clause gives both a beneficiary and the trustees of successor trusts the power to disclaim any property, and sets forth the manner in which the disclaimer should be exercised. Because state law may use terms other than disclaimer that have similar meaning, the terms renunciation and release also should be included. In addition, the trustees should be given the power to disclaim any power they are given under the instrument. For example, if a trustee is inadvertently given a power that would disqualify a trust for the marital deduction, or that unintentionally would cause the property to be taxable in the estate of the trustee, the trustee could disclaim the power and avoid the adverse tax consequences.

> **(N)** *Powers of Appointment. Any power of appointment created under this Agreement may be exercised only by an express reference to the power which includes my name, a general reference to this Agreement and reference to the applicable provisions of this Agreement. A person exercising a power of appointment may appoint trust funds outright or in further trust. Except to the extent otherwise expressly provided in this Agreement, the choice of terms, Trustee and jurisdiction of any appointive trust shall be entirely within the discretion of the person exercising the power of appointment. Notwithstanding any other provision of this Agreement to the contrary, no power of appointment shall be exercisable by a beneficiary over any property or its proceeds added to a trust by means of a disclaimer by such beneficiary.*

If the dispositive provisions of the trust give any beneficiary the power to direct how the property in the trust will be distributed, it is important to include specific restrictions on the manner of exercising the power. First, it is important to prevent an inadvertent exercise of a power of appointment. There can be significant adverse tax consequences to an exercise of a power of appointment. Under the majority common law rule, a power of appointment is not exercised merely by a residuary clause that refers to "all the rest, residue, and remainder of my property over which I have any interest." However, there are some circumstances where such broad language would be interpreted as a possible exercise of a power of appointment. This is even more likely to be true where the power of appointment is a general power of appointment.[91] To avoid any possibility that the power-holder inadvertently exercised the power of appointment, this clause requires an express reference to the name of the grantor, the trust instrument, and the specific provision granting the power.

The benefit of a power of appointment is to give the beneficiary holding the power the maximum flexibility to be as close to outright ownership as possible. The scope of the ability to exercise the power should be as broad as possible. The holder of the power should be given the ability to specify any terms for the exercise of the power, similar to the rights he would have as an outright owner of the property. The general common law allows the appointed property to continue in further trust. This savings clause does permit express exceptions to its broad terms for those circumstances where the grantor may prefer to limit the broad authority of the power-holder that is set forth in this clause.

The most important part of this clause is the final sentence. The preceding clause regarding disclaimer discusses some of the requirements to be a qualified disclaimer. However, another important criterion for a disclaimer to be a qualified disclaimer is that the property must pass without any direction from the disclaimant. If a beneficiary exercises a disclaimer over property and the property is added to a trust over which the disclaimant has a power of appointment, the disclaimer will not be qualified. For example, as discussed in the analysis of Section B.5 of Article V, the spouse may disclaim some property from the marital trust into the credit shelter trust in order to take advantage of some post-mortem tax planning. However, the credit shelter trust, as drafted, contains a power of appointment allowing the spouse to direct how the trust property will be distributed at the spouse's death. This power in the credit shelter trust would make the disclaimer into the marital trust a non-qualified disclaimer. The spouse could, and should, disclaim the power of appointment as well, but this option may be overlooked if the spouse acts without adequate tax advice. This savings clause will protect the disclaimer by providing that, notwithstanding the language of the credit shelter trust, the spouse will not have a power of appointment over the property that was added into the credit shelter trust by disclaimer.

---

[91] See the analysis of Section B.3 of Article V regarding the distinction between general and limited powers of appointment.

> **(O) *Investment Advisors.*** The Trustees may retain investment advisors; consult with such advisors on any matters relating to the retention, sale, purchase, investment, or reinvestment of securities or other property; delegate to such investment advisors the Trustees' investment authority; and pay such investment advisors reasonable compensation for their services. Such compensation shall be in addition to the regular compensation of the Trustees. The Trustees may act upon or refrain from acting upon the advice of such investment advisors in whole or in part. To the extent the Trustees follow the advice of such advisors or rely upon such investment advisor's exercise of delegated investment authority, the Trustees shall not be liable for any action taken or omitted, except in the case of willful misconduct.

Unless the trustee is a corporate trustee in the business of managing money, it is unlikely that the trustee will have the expertise necessary to manage trust funds. Historically, trustees could be held liable for poor investment performance regardless of their skills as investment managers. This created a distinct disadvantage to serving as trustee and had the unfortunate affect of causing trustees to be very conservative in their investment strategy. This served to benefit the current income beneficiaries to the disadvantage of future, remainder beneficiaries. This in turn led to further suits against trustees. The Uniform Principal and Income Act was adopted primarily to encourage trustees to invest for "total return." This allows the trustee to invest in a manner designed to maximize growth for the benefit of the remainder beneficiaries, as well as for the current income beneficiaries. There are many important provisions of the Uniform Principal and Income Act, but one of the most important provisions protects a trustee from liability if the trustee exercises reasonable care in the selection of a professional investment advisor, and delegates investment authority to that advisor. This was an important step to protect trustees that were not also professional money managers. This clause is designed to reiterate the provisions of the law and emphasize the grantor's intention to protect the trustee if the trustee reasonably relies on the advice of a professional investment advisor.[92] Section 807 of the Uniform Trust Code allows a trustee to delegate to an agent. The power to delegate requires the delegating trustee to use care in selecting the agent, and to periodically review the acts of the agent. If the trustee complies with these requirements, the trustee is protected from liability for acts of the agent.

Another important aspect of this clause is to allow the trustee to pay the investment advisor out of the trust funds. Traditionally, because managing the trust funds was an aspect of the trustee's duty, the trustee, at least in theory, would be required to pay an investment advisor out of his own fee. Such a rule might have the deleterious effect of encouraging the trustee to avoid hiring a professional investment advisor in order to avoid the reduction in the trustee's fees. This clause eliminates that potential conflict by providing that the investment advisor's fee is in addition to the trustee's fee.

> **(P)** *Delegation to Co-Trustee. Any Trustee may delegate to any co-Trustee any power or discretion that such co-Trustee is willing to accept. Such delegation shall be in writing, signed by the delegating Trustee and accepted by the Trustee to whom such delegation is made. Such writing shall set forth the duration of the period of delegation. Any person dealing with the Trustee may rely, without further inquiry, upon the statement of any Trustee as to any such Trustee's authority to act on behalf of any other Trustee.*

When there are multiple trustees, accomplishing administrative functions can be cumbersome. Allowing one trustee to delegate discretionary duties to another can be a convenience. The delegating trustee runs the risk that if the acting trustee breaches a fiduciary duty, the delegating trustee will be equally liable to the beneficiaries. Nonetheless, it is worthwhile to give the trustees the option to delegate to each other. The delegation is similar to a power of appointment, and if it is exercised, the scope of the delegation should be expressly set forth in writing.

---

[92] Not all states have adopted the Uniform Principal and Income Act. However, the majority of states have adopted it. Even if the applicable jurisdiction has not adopted the act, this clause should be sufficient in most states to accomplish the same result.

Line-by-Line Analysis 153

Allowing third parties to rely on the trustee's own statement regarding delegation of authority is designed to protect third parties who deal with the trustees. If the third party does not know he is protected in dealing with only one trustee, the third party will always require that all trustees participate in the proposed transaction. This would defeat the benefits of having this broad clause granting delegation of authority to one trustee. There is, of course, the risk that a trustee can misrepresent his authority. The trustee would be liable for such misrepresentation, but the innocent third party should not be liable. As a practical matter, most third parties would require at least written proof of delegation before relying on the assertion of authority by one trustee. The clause could be modified to require that the third party is protected only if he or she receives credible evidence of the delegation. However, such a limitation may prevent the third party from willingly accepting the authority of a single trustee.

> **(Q)** *Fiduciary Compensation.* Each Trustee acting hereunder shall be entitled to reasonable compensation for its services. Compensation shall be deemed reasonable if it is computed and paid in accordance with the schedule of rates (including minimum fees and additional compensation for special investments, closely held business interests and certain other services) published by the Trustee from time to time and in effect at the time the compensation is paid. If any individual acting as Trustee does not regularly publish a schedule of rates, then compensation to such Trustee shall be deemed reasonable if it is computed and paid in accordance with the average schedule of rates published by banks or trust companies for serving as professional Trustees in the community where the Trustee resides. Such compensation paid to a Trustee shall be deemed reasonable even if it is more or less than the statutory compensation for such services in effect from time to time under any applicable law.

Trustees are entitled to compensation for their service to the trust unless there is an express prohibition on the right to compensation. The work of a trustee, and the potential risk of liability for a trustee, are both substantial. A professional trustee would not serve without compensation. While friends or family may be willing to serve without compensation, the amount of work required of a trustee would make such a request unreasonable (unless the trustee also is a beneficiary). The root of most rules relating to compensation of fiduciaries is the notion that the fiduciary is entitled to receive reasonable compensation. However, the definition of reasonable varies widely from state to state. Some states set a statutory fee schedule that allows the trustee to obtain a fixed percentage of the value of the trust each year. The percentage typically is graduated with a higher percentage allowed for smaller trusts. If the trustee charges a fee based on the statutory schedule, it will be presumed to be reasonable. These statutory fee schedules typically permit an additional fee if the trustee is required to engage in extraordinary services, such as the management of a closely held business or dealing with trust-related litigation.

Other states do not have a statutory fee schedule that trustees can rely on to know whether the fees they charge are reasonable. Rather, those states tend to rely on case law that has developed a set of factors to consider when evaluating the reasonableness of the trustee's fee.[93] This lack of certainty can be problematic for trustees. Most corporate trustees have fee schedules that are similar to the statutory fee schedules. Individual professional trustees, such as attorneys or accountants, may have a percentage-based fee schedule, or they may prefer to charge in the traditional hourly rate manner for services performed. While the hourly rate charge compensates the trustee for work performed, it does not compensate for the substantial risk assumed by the trustee. If the trustee is not a professional, the trustee is unlikely to have a standard manner of charging for services and will be at a loss for how to determine a reasonable charge for services.

Whatever manner the trustee employees in setting its fee, a clause of this nature will protect the trustee who charges based on what the market will bear. A corporate or professional trustee who has a fee schedule is likely to be competitive with other corporate and professional trustees. A non-professional trustee can charge based on the average fee schedule of corporate trustees serving in the local area. This language will give trustees

---

[93] The case of *Hayward v. Plant*, 98 Conn. 374, (Conn. 1923), is an excellent example of a case law-driven analysis of the factors to be considered by courts in determining whether the trustee's fee is reasonable.

guidance as to the appropriate fees to charge. It also will give them a degree of confidence that if they so charge based on the community standard, their fees will be approved.

In addition to the benefits of providing guidance regarding fees, as a practical matter, most corporate and professional trustees will not serve as trustees if the trust does not contain broad approval in the governing instrument allowing them to charge based on their own fee schedules. In jurisdictions where there are statutory fee schedules, they tend to be very generous. It may not be advisable to encourage a trustee to adopt a fee schedule with higher rates. Even in a trust where only individual, non-professional trustees are contemplated, it is wise to incorporate provisions regarding payment of compensation to professional and corporate trustees. Circumstances may some day require the appointment of a professional or corporate trustee, and it will be easier to obtain a trustee where a provision regarding compensation already is included.

Article XIII

A will is not a will unless it is signed with a great deal of formality. Because the testator is no longer able to speak for himself when the will becomes operative, and because the will originally was the sole means of directing the transfer of wealth at death, these formalities make sense. In a way, the formalities themselves lend a degree of solemnity to the occasion and impress on the testator the importance of the act of making a will. A will, at minimum, usually must be signed by the testator and two witnesses who are not beneficiaries. The modern Law of Wills has created some exceptions, but the execution of wills remains formalistic. A will that is not validly executed cannot be probated, and the disposition under the will is void.

If a revocable living trust is a will substitute, the question arises of whether a revocable living trust must or should be executed with the same formality as a will. Historically, trusts have been treated more like contracts than wills with respect to the requirements of due execution. The key question is whether there is adequate evidence that the trust instrument was knowingly signed by the grantor with the intention of creating a trust. Because the law presumes that a person knows and understands what he signs, the simple signature of the grantor and the trustee should be enough to create a trust without any further formality. The Uniform Trust Code, in Section 601, requires that the requisite capacity of the grantor is the same as required for execution of the will. This encourages execution of revocable living trusts in a manner that is essentially identical to the requirements for execution of wills. Even in states that have not yet adopted the Uniform Trust Code, a statement setting forth the circumstances of the execution, as well as the presence of witnesses and a notary public, both provide useful evidence that the grantor actually signed the document and intended to create a trust. Thus, for all the reasons that wills require formal execution, prudence dictates equally formal execution of a revocable living trust.

Article XIII. *Due Execution.*

This Agreement shall not take effect until executed by me and at least one of the initial Trustees first named above, including myself. No successor or additional Trustee named herein or otherwise appointed pursuant to the terms of this Agreement shall be obligated to sign this instrument, nor shall a successor or additional Trustee who is duly appointed hereunder be required to sign a written acceptance of appointment as a Trustee. Notwithstanding the foregoing, each successor or additional Trustee acting hereunder, whether or not such Trustee signs a written acknowledgement of acceptance of appointment as successor or additional Trustee, shall be bound by the terms of this Agreement. This Agreement may be executed in several counterparts, each of which shall be deemed to be an original, but all of which together will constitute one and the same instrument.
WITNESS the due execution hereof by the parties hereto as of _____, 20__.

_____(L.S.)
JOHN J. DOE, *Grantor and Trustee*

Ideally, a trust agreement should be signed by all parties at the same time, as is required with wills. Where circumstances prevent one of the trustees from signing the agreement, that should not be fatal to the validity of the trust, so long as the grantor and at least one trustee signs. Also, it frequently happens that when one trustee ceases to act, by reason of death, resignation, or otherwise, his named successor merely steps in to act as trustee without going through the formality of signing a written acceptance of the appointment as trustee. This, too, should not be fatal to the validity of the trust, nor should it be used to invalidate any action taken by the successor trustee. The "due execution" clause makes clear that any successor trustee who serves is bound by the terms of the agreement, whether or not he signs anything agreeing to be bound by it. The clause also permits multiple originals of the same instrument, and allows the grantor and trustee to sign separate original. This can be helpful where the grantor and trustee are not together at the time of execution.

SIGNED, SEALED, PUBLISHED and DECLARED by JOHN J. DOE, the Grantor and Trustee, as and for his Revocable Trust, in the presence of us and each of us, who, at his request, in his presence and in the presence of each other, have hereunto subscribed our names as witnesses on _____, 20__.

_____

_____
Witness

_____

_____
Witness

I, Mary M. Doe, hereby accept appointment as Trustee of the John J. Doe Revocable Trust and acknowledge receipt of the foregoing instrument.

_____   _____
Witness   MARY M. DOE, *Trustee*

_____
Witness

STATE OF ANYSTATE   )

COUNTY OF ANYCOUNTY) : ss: Anytown
)

The foregoing instrument was acknowledged before me on _____, 2008, by JOHN J. DOE, *individually and as Trustee, who is personally known to me or who has produced adequate identification.*

_____
Notary Public

STATE OF ANYSTATE)
: ss: Anytown
COUNTY OF ANYCOUNTY)

The foregoing instrument was acknowledged before me on _____, 2008, by MARY M. DOE, *as Trustee, who is personally known to me or who has produced adequate identification.*

_____
Notary Public

The language preceding the signature of the witnesses is virtually identical to language that would be used as the attestation clause in a will. It sets forth what the instrument is (the John J. Doe Revocable Trust), who is signing it and why (John J. Doe as the grantor of the trust and as trustee, thereby accepting appointment as trustee), and the witnesses, who will acknowledge they were both present with the grantor when the grantor signed and when each of them signed as witnesses. This attestation will provide adequate evidence that the instrument was knowingly signed by the grantor and trustees as a revocable trust. The additional use of an acknowledgement before a notary public, or other officer authorized by state law to take an acknowledgement, provides further proof that the person signing was the named grantor and trustee.

Line-by-Line Analysis 159

The trustee also should accept appointment as trustee and acknowledge receipt of a copy of the trust agreement. While that is not necessary under the terms of the "due execution" clause, it is helpful to have proof of acceptance and receipt where possible to avoid later allegations of a lack of knowledge by any party.

Some Concluding Thoughts

After reviewing the clauses of the sample trust agreement and the line-by-line analysis of each, a few key points should be apparent. First, a great many of the trust provisions are tax-driven. In the absence of estate tax planning, the documents would be much simpler. However, this review has barely scratched the surface of the myriad tax issues involved in the most basic estate plan. If there is a possibility of tax liability, it is essential that the trust be drafted by a professional who understands all of the various implications of the estate and income tax laws.

The second important lesson is that the law in virtually all states, either by statute or case law, will provide a default rule on trust investment, management, distributions, and fiduciary responsibility when the trust agreement is silent. All a trust really needs is a trustee, a beneficiary, and an asset. The law can fill in all of the other gaps. However, the manner in which the law would fill those gaps may be inconsistent with what the grantor would have wanted. Historically, trust law gave great deference to the grantor and held the trustee to an almost impossibly high standard. As a result, the law was not particularly concerned with the rights of the beneficiaries. Modern trust law is reversing this trend by giving broader rights to the beneficiaries, moderating the liability of the trustee, and only giving a passing nod to the intent of the grantor if it can be clearly ascertained. Thus, if the grantor wants to maintain a degree of control, it is best to have a robust document that sets forth the grantor's intent with respect to all matters, however esoteric, rather than allowing the law to impose its own standards on the trust. Although there has been a movement to shorten trust documents by excluding matters and allowing the prevailing law to control, that may prove detrimental as the law continues to evolve.

Finally, the most important lesson of all is to select the trustee, and the mechanism for appointing successor trustees, with great care. Because trusts often are designed to last for many years, sometimes even multiple generations, flexibility is critical to success. Family circumstances and tax laws may change dramatically over time. The goals and objectives that once informed the creation of the trust may no longer apply. The trust must be flexible enough to allow the trustee to adapt to these changes. However, such flexibility can be abused in the hands of the wrong trustee. The trustee must have the ability to make the administrative decisions regarding the trust, including investment management and tax returns, as well as the distribution decisions. Sometimes the beneficiary is capable of filling both roles, but in many cases, the appointment of the beneficiary with an independent co-trustee not only may improve the quality of administration, but can aid in the objectives of tax savings and creditor protection. The independent trustee can make those decisions that are necessary to adapt the trust to the changing needs of the beneficiaries.

The sample trust clause and the analysis provide a starting point for drafting an effective trust. Customization options, both those that are discussed and some that have not been addressed, will allow the grantor to effectuate an estate plan that reduces exposure to probate and accomplishes appropriate wealth transfer, tax minimization, and creditor protection goals.

Appendix A: The Full Trust Agreement

REVOCABLE TRUST

OF

JOHN J. DOE

By and Between

JOHN J. DOE, as Grantor

and

JOHN J. DOE and MARY M. DOE, as Trustees

Dated

_____

This Revocable Trust Agreement was established in conjunction with a Will of the Grantor executed on the same day as this Revocable Trust Agreement. No change should be made to this Trust Agreement without a thorough review and analysis of the Grantor's Will and a determination of how any such change to this Revocable Trust Agreement may impact the Grantor's Will.

JOHN J. DOE REVOCABLE TRUST

This Trust Agreement is made on _____, 200__, by and between John J. Doe, now residing in Anytown, Anystate, as Grantor, and John J. Doe and Mary M. Doe, now residing in Anytown, Anystate, as Trustees.

WHEREAS, I desire to transfer, assign and convey Ten Dollars ($10.00) to the Trustees, together with any additional property acceptable to the Trustees that I or any other person may at any time transfer by beneficiary designation, assignment and delivery, or by gift, devise, bequest, appointment or otherwise, in order to establish a trust for the benefit of the beneficiaries named herein and for the purposes and subject to the terms and conditions set forth in this Agreement; and

WHEREAS, the Trustees acknowledge receipt of Ten Dollars ($10.00) and agree to hold said property, together with any additions thereto (hereinafter called the "trust estate"), in trust, for the purposes and subject to the terms and conditions set forth in this Agreement.

NOW THEREFORE, I establish this trust, which shall be known as the "John J. Doe Revocable Trust," and which shall be administered as follows:

Article XIV.   *Definition of Terms.*

As used in this Agreement, the following terms shall have the following meanings, unless otherwise expressly provided:

> **(A) *Identification of Spouse.*** *I am married to Mary M. Doe. Any reference to "my wife" or "my spouse" shall be a reference only to Mary M. Doe and shall not include any person to whom I was or may be married at any other time. If my marriage to Mary M. Doe is legally terminated by divorce, annulment, legal separation or otherwise, then for all purposes under this Agreement (including her appointment as a Trustee) Mary M. Doe (as well as any relative of hers who is not also a descendant of mine) shall be deemed to have died on the date of such termination.*
>
> **(B) *Identification of Children.*** *At present, my only children are Donald D. Doe and Debra D. Doe.*

(C) Definition of Children and Descendant. The terms "child," "children," "descendant" and "descendants," or any similar term, with respect to any person shall include such person's present biological children and descendants, as well as any children or other descendants born after the date of this Agreement. In addition, such term shall include any child or descendant legally adopted by such person, before or after the date of this Agreement; provided such child or descendant was adopted prior to attaining age eighteen (18).

(D) Definition of Education. The term "education," as used herein, shall include education at any level, including, but not limited to, preschool, elementary school, intermediate school, secondary school, college, graduate, post-graduate and professional training of any kind. It shall include, but is not necessarily limited to, the costs of tuition, fees imposed by any educational institution, books, supplies and the like. I intend that, under ordinary circumstances, the Trustees will interpret the term education liberally.

(E) Definition of Heirs-at-Law. The term "heirs-at-law" used with respect to any person shall mean those individuals (and in those proportions) to whom such person's Administrator would have been required to distribute such person's intestate estate if such person had then died intestate, unmarried, owning only such property and being a resident of Anystate.

(F) Definition of Per Stirpes. Notwithstanding the provision of any state's law to the contrary, whenever the Trustees are directed to distribute property to an individual's descendants or descendants "per stirpes," the property shall be divided into shares beginning with the first generation below such individual, whether or not there are members of such generation living at the time of distribution. Subdivision of shares for successive generations shall be made in the same manner.

(G) Definition of Trustee. Any reference to "the Trustee" or "the Trustees" shall encompass all Trustees then acting, including any Independent Trustee. The use of the singular shall be deemed to include the plural if there is more than one Trustee then acting, and the use of the plural shall include the singular if there is only one Trustee then acting. Any use of personal pronouns indicative of gender shall be deemed to include the masculine, feminine and neuter genders, as applicable. The Trustees also are sometimes referred to herein as *"fiduciaries."* Unless otherwise provided, any Trustee acting under this Agreement may exercise all of the rights, powers and discretions and shall be entitled to all of the privileges and immunities granted to the named Trustee.

(H) Definition of Professional Trustee. Any reference to a *"professional Trustee"* shall be limited to (i) a corporation or other entity authorized under the laws of the United States or of any state to administer trusts, (ii) a certified public accountant with expertise in trusts and estate matters who regularly provides services as a Trustee, or (iii) an attorney specializing in trusts and estate matters who regularly provides services as a fiduciary.

(I) Definition of Independent Trustee. For the purposes of this Agreement, a Trustee is an *"Independent Trustee"* only if such Trustee meets the following criteria: (i) is not a beneficiary currently eligible to receive the income or principal of the trust; (ii) is not a beneficiary who would be eligible to receive the income or principal of the trust if the trust were to terminate at the time the discretionary decision is made; (iii) is not the spouse, sibling, ancestor or descendant of a beneficiary described in subpart (i) or (ii); and (iv) in the case of any Trustee who is appointed by one or more of the beneficiaries described in subpart (i) or (ii), would not be a related or subordinate party with respect to any beneficiary who exercised the power to appoint such Trustee.

(J) Definition of Code. The term *"Code"* whenever used herein shall mean the Internal Revenue Code of 1986, as amended, or any corresponding provision of any subsequent Federal tax law, together with any regulations, proposed regulations or temporary regulations relating thereto.

(K) Definition of Related or Subordinate Party. The term *"related or subordinate party"* used with respect to any person shall have the same meaning as provided in section 672(c) of the Code, as if such person were the Grantor of the trust.

(L) Definition of Incapacity. An individual shall be considered to be incapacitated if the individual is (i) under a legal disability, or (ii) unable to give prompt and intelligent consideration to financial matters by reason of illness, mental or physical disability, disappearance or unaccountable absence. The determination as to whether an individual is incapacitated shall be made by the Trustees (other than such individual), or, if none, by the institution or individual designated to succeed such individual as Trustee, or, if none, by a majority of the beneficiaries then entitled to income of the trust. In making the determination, the Trustees may rely conclusively upon (i) the written opinion of either the individual's primary physician or any other two (2) board certified physicians (which certification is in the area of medicine most proximately related to the cause of the disability) stating that the individual is under a legal disability or is unable to give prompt and intelligent consideration to financial matters by reason of illness or mental or physical disability; (ii) the receipt of credible evidence that such individual has disappeared or is unaccountably absent; or (iii) the written order of any court. To enable the Trustees to obtain such opinions, I and all Trustees accepting their appointment as Trustee hereby waive any patient-doctor privilege or other privacy claims relating to information in the possession of any physician regarding such individual's mental or physical condition.

(M) *Definition of Death Taxes.* The term "death taxes," as used herein, shall mean any estate, transfer, excise, succession, inheritance, legacy, and other similar taxes (including any generation-skipping transfer tax, unless otherwise expressly provided) imposed by the federal government, any state, municipality, foreign government or any other tax authority by reason of my death. It also shall include any interest and penalties properly imposed thereon.

Article XV.   *Grantor Retained Rights.*

I reserve the right to amend or revoke this Agreement, and the estates and interests hereby created, in whole or in part. Any such revocation or amendment shall be in writing, signed and acknowledged by me, and delivered to each Trustee then acting. Notwithstanding the foregoing, the duties and obligations of the Trustees hereunder shall not be increased without their written consent. The rights under this Article are personal to me and may not be exercised by any person acting on my behalf in a fiduciary capacity.

Article XVI.   *Trust during My Lifetime.*

During my lifetime, the trust estate shall be administered as follows:

(A) *Distributions.* The Trustees shall pay to me or for my benefit so much or all of the net income and principal of the trust as I may request from time to time. If, in the opinion of the Trustees (other than me), or the named successor

Trustee if there is no other Trustee then acting, I am incapacitated, the Trustees may distribute to or for the benefit of me or my spouse so much or all of the net income and principal of the trust as the Trustees consider advisable to provide adequately for the education, maintenance in health and reasonable comfort, and support in accustomed manner of living of my spouse and me. The Trustees shall accumulate and add to principal at least annually any net income not so paid.

(B) *Limited Distributions to Agent for Gifts.* Without limiting the generality of the foregoing, if, in the opinion of the Trustees (other than me), or the named successor Trustee, if there is no other Trustee then acting, I am incapacitated, the Independent Trustee is specifically authorized to distribute to my agent or to any person or entity identified by my agent acting under a durable power of attorney executed by me such amounts as my agent specifically requests, in order to begin or continue any gift-giving program established by me. The power to make distribution to my agent shall be limited in scope and manner to permit the agent to make gifts in the manner expressly set forth in the durable power of attorney executed by me in favor of such agent.

(C) *Termination.* At my death, this trust shall terminate and any remaining property of the trust estate, together with any property added to the trust estate by reason of my death, shall be disposed of pursuant to Article IV of this Agreement.

Article XVII. *Disposition upon Death of Grantor.*

Any property directed to be disposed of pursuant to this Article shall be disposed of as follows:

(A) *Payment of Expenses, Debts and Taxes.*

1. *Payment to or for Executor.* The Trustees shall pay to or on behalf of the Executor of my estate or other personal representative ("the Executor"), out of the principal of the trust estate such amount or amounts as the Executor requests in writing for my funeral expenses, the expenses of administering my estate, any preresiduary gifts under my Will and any death taxes that are required by my Will to be paid as an administration expense. If an Executor is appointed to administer my

estate, the Trustees may rely conclusively on the written certification of the Executor as to the amount or amounts to be paid pursuant to this section.

2. **Direct Payment.** *If no Executor is appointed to administer my estate, the Trustees shall pay, out of the trust estate as an administration expense, my funeral expenses, the expenses of administering my estate, and any death taxes, other than any generation-skipping transfer tax, imposed upon or with respect to property that passes (i) under this Agreement, or (ii) from or under any retirement plan, trust or account (whether or not qualified under section 201, 403, 408 or 408A of the Code) that passes outright to or in trust for the benefit of my spouse and/or my descendants at my death.*

3. **Proration, Apportionment and Recovery.** *Any debts, death taxes or expenses that are directed to be paid out of the trust estate shall be paid without proration or apportionment against any beneficiary under this Agreement and without any statutory rights to recover any amounts so paid. All other death taxes not directed to be paid out of the trust estate as an administration expense pursuant to this section shall be prorated and apportioned in the manner provided by law with all applicable rights of recovery.*

4. **Debts.** *All property directed to be distributed pursuant to the terms of this Article (other than property disposed of as part of the Residuary Trust Estate) shall be distributed subject to any lien, mortgage or other debt secured by such property. Otherwise, the Trustees in their sole discretion may (but shall not be obligated to) pay out of the trust estate any and all of my enforceable debts that are due and payable; provided, however, that no such debts shall be paid out of assets that are exempt from creditors' claims.*

5. **Prohibited Use of Property.** *Notwithstanding any other provision of this section, the Trustees shall not use the proceeds of any qualified retirement plan or any property that is exempt from state or federal death taxes or the claims of other creditors that is held by or added to the trust estate by reason of my death to pay any debts, death taxes or expenses of administration pursuant to this section. The Trustees shall not contribute funds to my estate or make any payment directly or indirectly if such*

contribution or payment would subject to death taxes or the claims of other creditors property that otherwise would not be subject to such taxes or claims.

(B) Cash Bequest. The Trustees shall distribute Fifty Thousand Dollars ($50,000) to my sister, Betty Roe, if she survives me, otherwise this bequest shall lapse [*or:* otherwise to her descendants who survive me, per stirpes].

(C) Devise of Real Property. The Trustee shall distribute all of my real property [*or:* my real property located at 123 Main Street, Anytown, Anystate], together will all appurtenances thereto and buildings thereon, as well as any insurance related thereto, to my wife, if she survives me, otherwise this devise shall lapse.

(D) Tangible Personal Property. The Trustees shall distribute all of the tangible personal property (except cash, currency, coins and bullion) held or received by the Trustees at the time of my death as follows:

1. **Distributions.** Such property shall be distributed to my wife, if my wife survives me. If my wife does not survive me, such property shall be divided among my children who survive me, in such manner as they may agree. If my children cannot reach an agreement with respect to the disposition of such property within ninety (90) days after my death, or if any such child is then a minor or otherwise under a legal disability, then such property shall be divided by the Trustees in as nearly equal shares as practicble.

2. **Claims, Costs and Instructions.** Each beneficiary of tangible personal property under this section shall be entitled to any claims in my favor existing at my death with respect to the property distributed to such beneficiary, and, to the extent practical, shall be entitled to any insurance policies (or the proceeds of such policy if such proceeds become payable after my death) relating to such tangible personal property. Any costs of distribution of any tangible personal property, including, without limitation, storage, insurance, packing and delivery, shall be paid out of my general estate as an administrative expense. It is my request, without creating any legal obligation, that my Executors and family give due consideration to any separate instructions left by me for their guidance with respect to dividing and disposing of my tangible personal property.

(E) ***Disposition of Residuary Trust Estate.*** *The balance of the trust estate not otherwise disposed of by the preceding provisions of this Agreement and expressly including any lapsed or failed bequest or devise, (the "Residuary Trust Estate") shall be disposed of pursuant to Article IV of this Agreement.*

Article XVIII.   *Disposition of Residuary Trust Estate.*

The property to be disposed of pursuant to this Article shall be disposed of as follows:

(A) ***Credit Shelter Share.*** *If my wife survives me, the Trustees shall set aside the largest fractional share of the Residuary Trust Estate that may pass free of both federal estate tax and any state death tax imposed by reason of my death (referred to herein as the "Credit Shelter Share"), which share shall be determined and disposed of as follows:*

    1. ***Determination of Credit Shelter Share.*** *For purposes of this section, the largest fractional share of the Residuary Trust Estate that may pass free of federal estate tax imposed by reason of my death (the "federal credit share") shall be determined based only on the credit against estate taxes provided by section 2010 of the Code and the credit for state death taxes under section 2011 of the Code, if applicable, but only to the extent that it does not increase the death tax payable to any state. It shall be calculated by using the final determinations in the federal estate tax proceeding for my estate. The largest fractional share of the Residuary Trust Estate that will pass free of any state death tax imposed by reason of my death (the "state credit share") shall be determined by using the final determinations in each applicable state death tax proceeding for my estate. The term "state death tax" shall not include any generation-skipping transfer tax imposed by any state. In calculating either the federal credit share or the state credit share, each shall be calculated by deducting the amount of any such credit (including any credit for gift tax purposes) used by me during lifetime and by the amount of any such credit applied against property passing pursuant to any prior provision of this Agreement or outside this Agreement, and assuming that the balance of the Residuary Trust Estate qualifies for any marital deduction or exemption allowed by section 2056 of the Code or by any similar provision of any such state, regardless of whether all or any portion of it does in fact so qualify. There shall be allocated to the share to be disposed of under this section any* property that would not qualify for the federal estate tax marital deduction or any applicable state death tax marital deduction or exemption if allocated to the Residuary Marital Share.

2. **Distributions.** The Trustees shall hold the Credit Shelter Share in a separate trust hereunder (called the "Credit Shelter Trust") and may distribute so much or all of the net income and principal thereof to such one or more members of the class of individuals consisting of my wife and those of my descendants who are living from time to time during the term of the trust, in such shares and proportions, without requirement of equality, as the Trustees consider advisable to provide for the education, maintenance in health and reasonable comfort, and support in accustomed manner of living of any one or more of such individuals. In addition, the Independent Trustee may distribute so much or all of the net income and principal thereof to such one or more members of said class, in such shares and proportions, without requirement of equality, as the Independent Trustee considers advisable in its sole, absolute and uncontrolled discretion for any purposes whatsoever. The Trustees shall accumulate and add to principal at least annually any net income not so paid.

3. **Limitation on Distributions.** It is my request, without creating any legal obligation, that notwithstanding the foregoing no discretionary payment should be made from the principal of this trust to my wife unless and until all of the principal of the Marital Trust under section (B) of this Article has been completely paid out. The Trustees shall give first consideration to the needs of my wife before making distributions of income or principal of this trust to other eligible beneficiaries.

4. **Withdrawal Power.** In addition, the Trustees shall pay from the principal of the trust to my wife, upon written request, an amount that shall not exceed the greater of (i) Five Thousand Dollars ($5,000) or (ii) five percent (5%) of the principal of the trust (valued as of the first business day of the calendar year for which such withdrawal is available). This annual right to request withdrawal may be exercised only during the month of December, it shall be non-cumulative and it shall lapse at the end of such year to the extent it has not been exercised during the year. The power to withdraw principal under this subsection may be exercised

only by delivering a written request to the Trustees of this trust that specifically refers to this withdrawal power.

5. **Termination of Trust.** At the death of my wife, the Trustees shall distribute any remaining principal of this trust to or for the benefit of such individuals or charitable organizations, whatever terms and conditions, including in further trust, as my wife shall appoint by her Will, expressly referring to and exercising this power; provided, however, that this power shall be exercisable only in favor of a descendant of mine, if any descendant of mine is living, and, in any event, shall not be exercisable to any extent for the benefit of my wife, my wife's estate, or the creditors of either. Any such property not effectively appointed by my wife shall be disposed of pursuant to Article VI.

(B) **Residuary Marital Share.** If my wife survives me, the Trustees shall hold the balance of the Residuary Trust Estate in a separate trust hereunder (called the "Marital Trust") to be disposed of as follows:

1. **Distributions.** The Trustees shall pay or apply all of the net income thereof to or for the benefit of my wife at least annually. The Trustee also may pay or apply so much or all of the principal thereof as the Trustees consider advisable to provide for the maintenance in health and reasonable comfort, and support in accustomed manner of living of my wife. In addition, the Independent Trustee may distribute so much or all of the principal thereof to my wife as the Independent Trustee considers advisable in its sole, absolute and uncontrolled discretion for any purposes whatsoever.

2. **Withdrawal Power.** In addition, the Trustees shall pay from the principal of the trust to my wife, upon written request, an amount that shall not exceed the greater of (i) Five Thousand Dollars ($5,000) or (ii) five percent (5%) of the principal of the trust (valued as of the first business day of the calendar year for which such withdrawal is available). This annual right to request withdrawal may be exercised only during the month of December, it shall be noncumulative and it shall lapse at the end of such year to the extent it has not been exercised during the year. The power to withdraw principal under this subsection may be exercised only by

delivering a written request to the Trustees of this trust that specifically refers to this withdrawal power.

3. **Termination of Trust.** *At the death of my wife, the Trustees shall distribute any remaining principal of this trust to or for the benefit of such individuals or charitable organizations, whatever terms and conditions, including in further trust, as my wife shall appoint by her Will, expressly referring to and exercising this power; provided, however, that this power shall be exercisable only in favor of a descendant of mine, if any descendant of mine is living, and, in any event, shall not be exercisable to any extent for the benefit of my wife, my wife's estate, or the creditors of either. Any such property not effectively appointed by my wife shall be disposed of pursuant to Article VI.*

4. **Qualification for Marital Deduction.** *If my fiduciaries shall elect to qualify part or all of the property passing under this section for the state or federal estate tax marital deduction in my estate, no property shall be allocated to the Marital Trust that does not qualify for such marital deduction and, to the extent possible, no property shall be allocated to the Marital Trust as to which a foreign death tax credit is available. In addition, if my Executor shall elect to qualify part or all of the property passing under this section for the state or federal estate tax marital deduction in my estate, my spouse may, by written instrument, direct the Trustee to make any property held by the Marital Trust (including any property held in a retirement plan) productive of income within a reasonable time. This right is exclusive to my spouse and may not be exercised by any other person or entity. Whether or not my fiduciaries shall make such election, I intend to take advantage of the state and federal estate tax marital deductions, and all provisions of this Agreement shall be construed and all powers and discretion hereby conferred shall be exercised accordingly, anything in this Agreement to the contrary notwithstanding.*

5. **Disclaimer.** *If any portion of the Marital Share is disclaimed by my spouse or by the Trustees, such disclaimed property shall be added to the Credit Shelter Share.*

Appendix A: The Full Trust Agreement 173

(C) *Distribution if Grantor Survives.* If *my wife does not survive me, the Residuary Trust Estate shall be disposed of pursuant to Article VI.*

Article XIX. *Provisions for Descendants.*

Any property directed to be disposed of pursuant to this Article shall be divided into separate shares, per stirpes, with respect to my then living descendants, and such shares shall be disposed of as follows:

(A) *Distributions of Trust Property.* The Trustees shall hold the share of each such descendant (hereafter, the "Primary Beneficiary") in a separate trust hereunder. The Trustees may distribute so much or all of the net income and principal of each trust to one or more members of the class of individuals consisting of the Primary Beneficiary and his or her descendants who are living from time to time during the term of the trust, in such shares and proportions, without requirement of equality, as the Trustees consider advisable to provide for the education, maintenance in health and reasonable comfort, and support in accustomed manner of living of any one or more of such individuals. In addition, the Independent Trustee may distribute so much or all of the net income and principal thereof to one or more members of such class, in such shares and proportions, without requirement of equality, as the Independent Trustee considers advisable in its sole, absolute and uncontrolled discretion for any purposes whatsoever. The Trustees shall accumulate and add to principal at least annually any net income not so paid. The Trustees shall give first consideration to the needs of the Primary Beneficiary before making distributions to other eligible beneficiaries.

(B) *Primary Beneficiary Withdrawal Rights.* After attaining each of the following ages, the Primary Beneficiary shall have the cumulative right to withdraw from the trust principal an amount equal to the following fractions of the value of the trust (as well as the following fractions of the value of any subsequent additions to the trust principal, as of the date of the addition): (i) one-third (1/3) after reaching the age of thirty (30) years; (ii) one-half (1/2) after reaching the age of thirty-five (35) years; and (iii) all or any part of the remaining value of the trust after reaching the age of forty (40) years. This right shall be cumulative and shall be exercisable as of the date the Primary Beneficiary attains such age or as of such date as the Primary Beneficiary's trust is funded, if later. The fractions hereunder shall be calculated by reducing such value by any amount which could have been withdrawn earlier but was not. The power to withdraw principal hereunder may be exercised only by delivery of a written instrument to the Trustees of such trust, or by a Will, specifically referring to the withdrawal power.

(C) *Limited Power of Appointment.* At the death of the Primary Beneficiary, the Trustees shall distribute any remaining principal of the trust to or for the benefit of such individuals or charitable organizations, on whatever terms and conditions, including in further trust, as the Primary Beneficiary shall appoint by his or her Will, expressly referring to and exercising this power; provided, however, that this power shall be exercisable only in favor of a descendant of mine, if any descendant of mine is living, and, in any event, shall not be exercisable to any extent for the benefit of the Primary Beneficiary, his or her estate, or the creditors of either.

(D) *Disposition of Remaining Trust Property.* Any remaining trust principal not effectively appointed by the Primary Beneficiary shall be divided into separate shares, per stirpes, with respect to the then living descendants of the Primary Beneficiary, if any. If the Primary Beneficiary has no descendants then living, such property shall be divided into separate shares, per stirpes, with respect to the then living descendants of the nearest ancestor of the Primary Beneficiary who also is a descendant of mine, if any, or if none, such property shall be divided into separate shares, per stirpes, with respect to my then living descendants. If I have no descendants then living, such property shall be disposed of pursuant to the Article entitled Family Disaster. Any share determined pursuant to this section shall be added to the trust, if any, of which such descendant is a Primary Beneficiary under this Article, or, if none, shall be held by the Trustees in a separate trust for such descendant pursuant to this Article.

Article XX. *Family Disaster.*

If, upon the termination of any trust hereunder, any property is not effectively disposed of by any other provision of this Agreement, or if any property is directed to be disposed of pursuant to this Article, as the case may be, such property shall be distributed as follows: one-half (1/2) to my heirs-at-law and one-half (1/2) to my spouse's heirs-at-law [or: to ABC Charity, Inc. for its general, tax-exempt use and purposes].

Appendix A: The Full Trust Agreement

Article XXI.   *Spendthrift Provision.*

One of my primary purposes in establishing this trust is to protect the trust estate from claims of the beneficiaries' creditors and to protect the assets from the improvidence of any beneficiary. Accordingly, the income and principal of any trust hereunder shall be used only for the personal benefit of the designated beneficiaries of the trust, and no distributions or expenditures of trust assets shall be made except to or for the benefit of such beneficiary. To the maximum extent permitted by law, a beneficiary's interest in the income and principal of this trust shall not be subject to voluntary or involuntary transfer. Without in any way limiting the generality of the foregoing: (i) no beneficiary shall have any right to anticipate, transfer or encumber any part of any interest in the trust estate; (ii) no beneficiary's interest shall be liable for such beneficiary's debts or obligations (including alimony) or be subject to attachment, levy, or other legal process; and (iii) each beneficiary's interest in the trust estate shall constitute the separate property of the beneficiary and shall be free from any right, title, interest, or control of the beneficiary's spouse.

Article XXII.   *Termination of Trusts.*

Anything in this Agreement to the contrary notwithstanding, the Independent Trustee is authorized to terminate any trust under this Agreement if the Independent Trustee determines, in its sole, absolute and uncontrolled discretion, that it is not economical or otherwise in the best interests of the beneficiaries of such trust to keep such trust in existence. The decision of the Independent Trustee to terminate or not to terminate any trust hereunder shall be binding and conclusive upon all persons interested in such trust, and, to the extent permitted by law, is not subject to review by any court or administrative tribunal. The determination of whether it is economical to maintain a trust shall be made without regard to any statutory provision with respect to the termination of "small" trusts. In making the determination of whether to terminate any trust hereunder, the Independent Trustee shall give primary consideration to the interests of the current eligible income beneficiaries of such trust. Upon the termination of any trust pursuant to this Article, the Independent Trustee shall distribute any remaining income and principal of such trust to any one or more of the current eligible income beneficiaries of the terminating trust as the Independent Trustee, in its sole, absolute and uncontrolled discretion considers advisable; provided, however, that the Independent Trustee may, in its sole, absolute and uncontrolled discretion, elect to distribute the remaining trust property to a separate trust for the benefit of any one or more of the current eligible income beneficiaries of the *terminating trust upon whatever terms and conditions the Independent Trustee deems advisable.*

Article XXIII. *Trustees Provisions.*

The following provisions shall apply with respect to the appointment and service of the Trustees:

> **(A)** ***Initial Trustee.*** *My spouse and I shall be the initial co-Trustees hereunder. If either my spouse or I is incapacitated, the other may act as sole Trustee. My spouse shall act as a Trustee of any trust of which my spouse is a beneficiary.*
>
> **(B)** ***Appointment of Successor Trustees.*** *My sister, BETTY ROE, is appointed as a Trustee of each trust hereunder, to act together with any other then acting Trustee, upon the first to occur of: (i) my death [**or:** the death of the survivor of my wife and me], (ii) appointment by me, or (iii) a complete vacancy in the office of Trustee, including by reason of the incapacity of all of the then-acting Trustees. If BETTY ROE fails to qualify or ceases to act as Trustee, her husband, ROBERT ROE, is appointed as a Trustee, to act together with any other then-acting Trustee.*
>
> **(C)** ***Primary Beneficiary as Trustee.*** *The Primary Beneficiary of each trust under Article V, who has attained the age of twenty-one (21) years, is appointed as a Trustee of such trust, to act together with any other then-acting Trustee.*
>
> **(D)** ***Additional and Successor Trustees.*** *After my death or if I am incapacitated, any Trustee then acting is authorized to appoint an additional Trustee or Trustees or a successor Trustee or a succession of successor Trustees to act in the event of any vacancy in his or her office not otherwise provided for above. If, in the event of any vacancy in the office of Trustee, no successor has been named herein or appointed as hereinabove provided, then the following individuals (or groups) who are willing and able to act, in the order listed, may appoint one or more successor Trustees of such trust: (i) my spouse, if living and not then incapacitated; (ii) the Primary Beneficiary of such trust, if any, and if not then incapacitated; (iii) a majority of the other eligible income beneficiaries of such trust who are not then incapacitated; or (iv) a majority of my then-living adult children who are not then incapacitated. If any vacancy in the office of*

Appendix A: The Full Trust Agreement

Trustee is not otherwise adequately filled by the foregoing provisions, a court of competent jurisdiction may appoint a successor Trustee. If any Trustee who is or would be an Independent Trustee fails to qualify or ceases to act as a Trustee, and a successor Trustee is appointed pursuant to the terms of this section, such successor Trustee shall qualify only if such successor so named will qualify as an Independent Trustee.

(E) ***Removal and Replacement by Grantor.*** I may at any time and for any reason remove and replace any Trustee, including my spouse, and may name additional or successor Trustees, without regard to any additional or successor Trustee(s) otherwise named herein.

(F) ***Removal and Replacement by Spouse.*** After my death, or if I become incapacitated, then my spouse (if not then incapacitated) shall have the right to remove any Trustee of any trust hereunder and may, but is not obligated to, appoint one or more successor Trustees (other than my spouse) without regard to the appointment of any successor otherwise named hereunder; provided, however, that the successor Trustee so appointed would not be a related or subordinate party subservient to the wishes of my spouse.

(G) ***Removal and Replacement by Primary Beneficiary.*** The Primary Beneficiary of any trust established under Article V of this Agreement who has attained the age of twenty-one (21) years and who is not incapacitated shall have the right to remove any Trustee of such trust and to appoint one or more successor Trustees (other than himself or herself) without regard to the appointment of any successor otherwise named hereunder; provided, however, that the successor Trustee so appointed shall be a professional Trustee who would not be a related or subordinate party subservient to the wishes of the Primary Beneficiary.

(H) ***Resignation of Trustee.*** Any Trustee may resign at any time without the approval of any court by giving written notice of resignation to me, if I am living and not then incapacitated, or to the adult eligible income beneficiaries of the trust, to each co-Trustee, and to each Trustee to be appointed; provided, however, that if no co-Trustee is then acting, such resignation shall become effective only upon the qualification of a successor fiduciary. If a Trustee is incapacitated, such Trustee shall be deemed to have resigned as of the date of the determination of incapacity.

(I) *Procedure for Resignation, Appointment and Removal.* The appointment, revocation of appointment or removal of a Trustee shall be made by delivery of a written, acknowledged instrument to the then-acting Trustees and any Trustee to be appointed. Any appointment of a Trustee may be conditioned to commence or cease upon a future event and may be revoked or modified by the individuals or entity entitled to make such appointment at any time prior to the occurrence of such event. Unless otherwise expressly provided, any power to appoint a Trustee shall permit appointment of an individual or a corporation or other entity authorized under the laws of the United States or of any state to administer trusts as Trustee. Any power to appoint, but not a power to remove, shall be exercisable by the legal representative of any disabled person holding such power (including the parent acting as natural guardian of any minor beneficiary).

(J) *Bond.* No bond or other security shall be required of any Trustee at any time acting for any purpose or in any jurisdiction.

(K) *Exoneration of Trustee.* Any individual who is related to me (whether by blood or through marriage) who is serving as a Trustee shall not be liable for any mistake or error of judgment, or for any action taken or omitted, either by the Trustee or by any agent or attorney employed by the Trustee, or for any loss or depreciation in the value of the trust, except in the case of willful misconduct. No Trustee has a duty to examine the transactions of any prior Trustee, and each Trustee is responsible only for those assets that actually are delivered to the Trustee.

Article XXIV.   *Trustee Powers.*

Without limiting any other powers granted by this Agreement or authorized by law, the Trustees shall have the following powers and discretions, which shall extend to all principal and income held hereunder in any capacity or for any purpose (including accumulated income) until the final and outright distribution thereof, and which the Trustees may exercise with sole, absolute and uncontrolled discretion, without application to or approval by any court:

(A) To retain, acquire or sell any variety of real or personal property (including any discretionary common trust fund of any corporate fiduciary acting under this document, mutual funds, covered or uncovered stock options, insurance policies on *my life and investments in foreign securities), without regard to diversification and without being limited to the investments authorized for trust funds;*

(B) *To enter into agreements for the sale, merger, reorganization, dissolution or consolidation of any property, including corporation or other business entity;*

(C) *To manage, improve, repair, sell, mortgage, lease (including the power to lease for oil and gas), pledge, convey, option or exchange any property and take back purchase money mortgages thereon;*

(D) *To open, close, maintain, draw checks on or otherwise withdraw funds from, and make deposits into bank accounts of any kind;*

(E) *To maintain custody or brokerage accounts (including margin accounts) and to register securities in the name of a nominee;*

(F) *To exercise stock options;*

(G) *To vote and give proxies to vote shares of stock, interest in a partnership, membership interest in a limited liability company or any similar business interest;*

(H) *To make joint investments in any property, whether real or personal; to enter into and act as a general or limited partner in general or limited partnerships; to establish corporations (including limited liability companies) of any kind; and to transfer assets to any such joint ventures, partnerships or corporations;*

(I) *To serve as an officer or director of any business entity owned, in whole or in part, by any trust hereunder;*

(J) *To compromise and settle all claims by or against any trust or trust property hereunder (including those relating to taxes);*

(K) *To borrow funds from any person or entity (including a Trustee hereunder) and to pledge or mortgage trust assets to secure such loans;*

(L) *To extend, renew or renegotiate loans or guarantees;*

(M) *To lend money to or for the benefit of any person beneficially interested hereunder (including a Guardian);*

(N) *To divide any trust hereunder into separate trusts based on the fair market value of the trust assets at the time of the division;*

(O) *To administer multiple trusts established under this document in solido; and*

(P) *To exercise in good faith and with reasonable care all other investment and administrative powers and discretions of an absolute owner that lawfully may be conferred upon a fiduciary.*

Article XXV. *Administrative Provisions.*

The following additional provisions shall apply to all trusts created hereunder:

(A) Presumption of Survival. *No successor beneficiary shall be deemed to have survived the event creating a present interest hereunder in the successor beneficiary unless such beneficiary survives such event by more than thirty (30) days. Notwithstanding the foregoing, my spouse shall be deemed to have survived me if my spouse survives me for any period of time or if the order of our deaths cannot be determined.*

(B) Anti-lapse Provision. *If any disposition under this Agreement is contingent upon the survival of a beneficiary and the beneficiary does not satisfy the condition of survival, and if there is no substitute taker designated who satisfies the conditions for taking, such disposition shall lapse. The provisions of any anti-lapse statute in any jurisdiction shall not apply to preserve any disposition to or for the benefit of any individual who is not identified as a substitute taker hereunder.*

(C) Additional Provisions for Payment of Income and Principal. *The following provisions shall apply with respect to the payment of income or principal from each trust hereunder:*

    1. *Income payments shall be paid at least annually unless accumulation of income is authorized, or some shorter period is expressly provided.*

Appendix A: The Full Trust Agreement

2. *Unless otherwise expressly provided, upon the occurrence of any event causing termination of any trust, any accrued and collected, but undistributed income shall be added to principal.*

3. *The Trustees may, without the approval of any court, make distributions of income and principal in cash or in kind, or partly in each, and, may, in their discretion, allocate particular assets or portions thereof to any one or more beneficiaries, without any duty to distribute any asset pro rata among beneficiaries. The Trustees may do so without regard to the income tax basis of specific property allocated to any beneficiary, provided that such property shall be valued for purposes of distribution at its value on the date of distribution.*

4. *Whenever provision is made for distribution of principal or income to any person, the same may instead be applied for the benefit of such person. Application of principal or income for the benefit of a person under any legal disability may be made by payment to or application for the use of such person directly, or in the discretion of the Trustees by payment to such person's parent, spouse, custodian under any gifts or transfers to minors act, guardian, committee or conservator, in whatever jurisdiction appointed, or any one with whom such person resides, and the receipt of the one to whom any such distribution is made shall be a full discharge from accountability to such person. The decision of the Trustees as to the purpose, time and amount of any payment of income or principal shall be binding and conclusive upon all beneficiaries of this Agreement.*

5. *Notwithstanding any other provision of this Agreement or applicable law to the contrary, after my death, or if I am incapacitated, any Trustee who is not an Independent Trustee shall not participate in any discretionary decision unless the discretionary decision is limited by an ascertainable standard as defined in section 2041(b) of the Code and the Regulations thereunder. As used herein, a "discretionary decision" includes any decision regarding the distribution, payment, application, accumulation, or allocation of income or principal, or the termination of a trust. In making any discretionary decision concerning the distribution of trust property the Trustees may (but shall not be required to) take into consideration other resources reasonably available to the beneficiary eligible to receive the distribution.*

(D) *Provisions for Retirement Assets in a Marital Trust.* If any trust of which my spouse is the sole income beneficiary is named as the beneficiary of a qualified retirement plan, the Trustees of such trust shall withdraw during the calendar year from the qualified retirement plan an amount equal to the greatest of: (i) the minimum required distribution for the calendar year; (ii) the income generated or deemed to be generated by the assets in the retirement plan for the year; and (iii) the portion of the retirement plan that is treated as trust income for such year under the state law applicable to the administration of such trusts. The Trustee shall distribute to my spouse, as income, an amount that is no less than the greater of (i) the income generated or deemed to be generated by the assets in the retirement plan for the year, or (ii) the portion of the retirement plan that is treated as trust income for such year under the state law applicable to the administration of such trust. No expenses chargeable to principal under applicable state law shall be charged against the income earned by the qualified retirement plan and withdrawn by the Trustees.

(E) *Additions to and Combination of Trusts.* If, upon the termination of any trust, any property is set aside in respect of a person for whom another trust is then held hereunder, then such property shall instead be added to the principal of such other trust and administered and disposed of as an integral part thereof. The Independent Trustees may, in their sole, absolute and uncontrolled discretion, combine any trust under this Agreement with any other substantially identical trust established by either or both of my spouse and me. A trust may be deemed to be substantially identical to a trust hereunder notwithstanding that the perpetuities vesting period of such other trust may be shorter or longer than the trust hereunder, and the Independent Trustee may combine such trusts, provided that the trust thereby surviving shall take the shorter perpetuities vesting period.

(F) *Governing Law and Situs.* The validity, construction and administration of this Agreement and any trust hereunder shall be governed by the laws of Anystate. The Trustees, at any time and for any reason, may transfer the place of administration and assets of any trust to any jurisdiction. It is my expectation and intention that no court approval will be required for such a transfer. However, the Trustees may seek court approval of such transfer if necessary, and I expect the court to approve the transfer as such is consistent with my intent. The Independent Trustees may change the governing law to any jurisdiction at any time and for any reason, provided that a change in the place of administration shall not result in a change in the governing law unless specifically directed by the Independent Trustees. The Independent Trustees may make technical amendments to this Agreement to make any transferred trust valid and effective under the laws of the transferee jurisdiction.

(G) **Trust Distributions to Guardians.** *If my spouse is deceased and if the Trustees are authorized to distribute the income or principal of any trust under this Agreement to a child of mine who is a minor, the Trustees may apply such income and principal for the benefit of such child by making unconditional distributions to such child's Guardians if, in my Trustees' judgment, such distributions would have an indirect but substantial benefit to such child. For example, I would consider it suitable for the Trustees to assist the Guardians in acquiring a larger home if needed to accommodate my child, to pay for needed housekeeping and childcare services, or to help defray the costs of family vacations for the Guardians' family with my child. The Trustees may retain the family home and permit the Guardians' family to live in such home during the period of guardianship or for as long as the Guardians continue to provide a home for such child. If any Guardian is also acting as a Trustee of such trust, such Guardian shall not participate in any discretionary accumulation, payment, distribution, application or allocation of income or principal under this section.*

(H) **Legal Obligations.** *The trust estate hereunder shall remain available to satisfy any of my legal obligations during my lifetime. Except with respect to the foregoing, no provision of this Agreement shall be construed as relieving any person of his or her legal obligations, including the obligation to support any beneficiary hereunder. No part of the income or principal of any trust hereunder and no exercise of a power of appointment granted herein shall be used to satisfy any such legal obligations.*

(I) **Rule Against Perpetuities.** *Each trust hereunder shall terminate upon the expiration of twenty-one (21) years following the death of the survivor of me, my spouse and those of my descendants who are living on the date of my death. At the expiration of such perpetuities vesting period, the Trustees shall pay any remaining income and principal of such trust to the Primary Beneficiary, or, if none, to the then living descendants, per stirpes, of the Primary Beneficiary, or, if none, to my then living descendants, per stirpes, who are eligible income beneficiaries of the trust.*

(J) Outright Distributions to Minors. *If, upon the termination of any trust, any property vests absolutely and free of trust in a minor, and is not otherwise directed to be retained in further trust for such minor under any other provision of this Agreement, then the Trustees may distribute the same to any custodian for such minor under any gifts or transfers to minors act. The Trustees may designate as custodian any person, including any one of the Trustees, who is qualified to act in such capacity. In the alternative, the Trustees may retain and manage the same during the beneficiary's minority, without bond and with all powers and discretion granted to the Trustees by this Agreement or by law. The Trustees may pay or apply the income and principal of such trust for the health, education, support or maintenance of such minor, accumulating any income not so applied, until such minor reaches the age of majority (pursuant to the laws of the jurisdiction where the beneficiary is domiciled) or until the prior death of such minor. At such time, any remaining principal and accumulated income shall be paid to such minor or to his or her estate.*

(K) Tax Elections. *The Trustees and/or the Executor of my estate, in their sole discretion and without the order or approval of any court, are authorized to make or not make any election, allocation or other discretionary decision permitted under the provisions of any tax law in effect from time to time. My fiduciaries also may make or decline to make equitable adjustments of the interests of the beneficiaries in light of such decisions. Notwithstanding the foregoing grant of discretion, my fiduciaries shall make any adjustment necessary to avoid reducing any marital deduction under any tax law. The Trustees may, except with respect to any trust under this document in which my spouse is the sole income beneficiary, allocate property (or the right to receive property) which is subject to estate tax and federal income tax as income in respect of a decedent to principal, to income, or in part to each. No beneficiary shall have any rights against any fiduciary by reason of any such decisions or adjustments.*

(L) Trust Accountings. *While the trust holds asset worth less than one hundred dollars ($100), the Trustee shall make no accounting. The Trustees may, in their sole discretion, settle any account at any time by agreement or judicially. Any agreement made with those beneficiaries under no legal disability who at the time are currently entitled to the income or presumptively entitled to the principal shall bind all individuals, whether or not then in being or of legal* capacity, then or thereafter entitled to the income or principal, and shall release and discharge the Trustees for the acts and proceedings embraced in the account as effectively as a judicial settlement, notwithstanding the circumstance that any Trustee may also be a party to such agreement in a separate capacity, either individually or as a fiduciary of another estate or trust. The Trustees may provide to me, or my guardian or conservator if I am incapacitated, or, after my death, to each eligible income beneficiary and presumptive remainderman (or the parent or legal representative of any such individual who is a minor or is incapacitated), statements of trust transactions at such time and in such form as the Trustees consider advisable. If all such individuals either give written approval of the statement or fail to notify the Trustees in writing of any objection within thirty (30) days of the mailing of the statement to such individuals, the statement shall be final, binding and conclusive on all individuals interested in the trust, regardless of whether such statements would qualify as an accounting pursuant to local law.

(M) *Virtual Representation.* Where a party to any judicial proceeding or agreement (whether or not related to the accounts of my Trustees) has the same or a similar interest as a person under a disability (including by reason of minority), or where a beneficiary may not yet be born or ascertained, it shall not be necessary to serve the person under a disability, or to make such person a party to the agreement, nor shall it be necessary to appoint a guardian ad litem, or similar fiduciary, to represent the interests of any such disabled, unborn or unascertained beneficiary.

(N) *Generation-Skipping Transfer Tax Provisions.*

1. The Trustees and/or my Executor may allocate any portion of my federal generation-skipping transfer tax exemption to any property as to which I am the transferor, including any property transferred by me prior to my death. The Independent Trustees also may divide any trust into two separate trusts based on the fair market value of the trust assets at the time of the division, so that the federal generation-skipping transfer tax inclusion ratio for each such trust shall be either zero or one. Such division shall be based on the fair market value of the trust assets at the time of division. The Independent Trustees may allocate additions to any trust so that all trusts or property with an inclusion ratio of zero are allocated to a trust hereunder with an inclusion ratio of zero and all trusts or property

with an inclusion ratio of one are allocated to a trust hereunder with an inclusion ratio of one.

2. Any reference to my federal generation-skipping transfer tax exemption shall mean the exemption provided for by section 2631 of the Code that has not been allocated by me, by my fiduciaries or by operation of law to property transferred by me during my lifetime or allocated by my fiduciaries to property passing by reason of my death, whether outside this Agreement or under any Article of this Agreement that precedes the disposition of the Residuary Trust Estate.

3. The term "inclusion ratio" shall have the same meaning as provided in section 2642 of the Code. As used herein, I intend that any reference to a trust having an inclusion ratio of zero shall mean that the trust is exempt from the generation-skipping transfer tax, and any trust that has an inclusion ratio greater than zero shall mean a trust that is subject to generation-skipping transfer tax, in whole or in part.

4. At the death of the Primary Beneficiary of a trust established under this Agreement, if any trust property would pass to or in trust for the descendants of the Primary Beneficiary, then the Primary Beneficiary shall have a general power of appointment limited to the following terms. Such power shall be a power to appoint to the Primary Beneficiary's estate by a Will expressly referring to and exercising such power, the smallest fractional share of such trust property that would reduce to a minimum the aggregate estate, inheritance, succession and generation-skipping transfer taxes payable by reason of the Primary Beneficiary's death. Such fractional share shall be determined as if any power of appointment of the Primary Beneficiary (under this provision or otherwise) is not exercised and the trust principal and the Primary Beneficiary's entire gross estate for federal estate tax purposes are to be distributed to the Primary Beneficiary's descendants.

(O) **Disclaimers.** Any person (or his or her attorney-in-fact or legal representative, including the executor, administrator, conservator or other personal representative of his or her estate) may irrevocably disclaim, renounce or release any interest, benefit, right, privilege or power granted to such person or entity under this Agreement, in whole or in part, without approval of any court.

Further, with regard to any interest in property passing to any trust under this Agreement (including a beneficial interest in a trust) or any fiduciary power under this Agreement, the Trustees may irrevocably disclaim, renounce or release any such interest, benefit, right, privilege or power, , in whole or in part, without the approval of any court. Any such disclaimer, renunciation or release shall be in writing, signed by the disclaimant, renouncer or releaser in the presence of two disinterested witnesses and shall be duly acknowledged before a proper official for taking acknowledgments and shall comply with any other applicable requirements of local, state and federal law regarding the formalities of execution and delivery of such instruments.

(P) Powers of Appointment. Any power of appointment created under this Agreement may be exercised only by an express reference to the power which includes my name, a general reference to this Agreement and reference to the applicable provisions of this Agreement. A person exercising a power of appointment may appoint trust funds outright or in further trust. Except to the extent otherwise expressly provided in this Agreement, the choice of terms, Trustee and jurisdiction of any appointive trust shall be entirely within the discretion of the person exercising the power of appointment. Notwithstanding any other provision of this Agreement to the contrary, no power of appointment shall be exercisable by a beneficiary over any property or its proceeds added to a trust by means of a disclaimer by such beneficiary.

(Q) Investment Advisors. The Trustees may retain investment advisors; consult with such advisors on any matters relating to the retention, sale, purchase, investment, or reinvestment of securities or other property; delegate to such investment advisors the Trustees' investment authority; and pay such investment advisors reasonable compensation for their services. Such compensation shall be in addition to the regular compensation of the Trustees. The Trustees may act upon or refrain from acting upon the advice of such investment advisors in whole or in part. To the extent the Trustees follow the advice of such advisors or rely upon such investment advisor's exercise of delegated investment authority, the Trustees shall not be liable for any action taken or omitted, except in the case of willful misconduct.

(R) Delegation to Co-Trustee. Any Trustee may delegate to any co-Trustee any power or discretion that such co-Trustee is willing to accept. Such delegation shall be in writing, signed by the delegating Trustee and accepted by the Trustee to whom such delegation is made. Such writing shall set forth the duration of the period of delegation. Any person dealing with the Trustee may rely, without further inquiry, upon the statement of any Trustee as to any such Trustee's authority to act on behalf of any other Trustee.

(S) *Fiduciary Compensation.* Each Trustee acting hereunder shall be entitled to reasonable compensation for its services. Compensation shall be deemed reasonable if it is computed and paid in accordance with the schedule of rates (including minimum fees and additional compensation for special investments, closely held business interests and certain other services) published by the Trustee from time to time and in effect at the time the compensation is paid. If any individual acting as Trustee does not regularly publish a schedule of rates, then compensation to such Trustee shall be deemed reasonable if it is computed and paid in accordance with the average schedule of rates published by banks or trust companies for serving as professional Trustees in the community where the Trustee resides. Such compensation paid to a Trustee shall be deemed reasonable even if it is more or less than the statutory compensation for such services in effect from time to time under any applicable law.

Article XXVI. *Due Execution.*

This Agreement shall not take effect until executed by me and at least one of the initial Trustees first named above, including myself. No successor or additional Trustee named herein or otherwise appointed pursuant to the terms of this Agreement shall be obligated to sign this instrument, nor shall a successor or additional Trustee who is duly appointed hereunder be required to sign a written acceptance of appointment as a Trustee. Notwithstanding the foregoing, each successor or additional Trustee acting hereunder, whether or not such Trustee signs a written acknowledgement of acceptance of appointment as successor or additional Trustee, shall be bound by the terms of this Agreement. This Agreement may be executed in several counterparts, each of which shall be deemed to be an original, but all of which together will constitute one and the same instrument.

Appendix A: The Full Trust Agreement

WITNESS the due execution hereof by the parties hereto as of _____, 20___.

_____(L.S.)
JOHN J. DOE, Grantor and Trustee

SIGNED, SEALED, PUBLISHED and DECLARED by JOHN J. DOE, the Grantor and Trustee, as and for his Revocable Trust, in the presence of us and each of us, who, at his request, in his presence and in the presence of each other, have hereunto subscribed our names as witnesses on _____, 20___.

_____   _____
                                            Witness

_____   _____
                                            Witness

I, Mary M. Doe, hereby accept appointment as Trustee of the John J. Doe Revocable Trust and acknowledge receipt of the foregoing instrument.

_____   _____
Witness   MARY M. DOE, Trustee

_____   _____
                                            Witness

STATE OF ANYSTATE   )
                         : ss: Anytown
COUNTY OF ANYCOUNTY   )

The foregoing instrument was acknowledged before me on _____, 20___, by JOHN J. DOE, *individually and as Trustee, who is personally known to me or who has produced adequate identification.*

_____
Notary Public

STATE OF ANYSTATE   )
                         : ss: Anytown
COUNTY OF ANYCOUNTY   )

The foregoing instrument was acknowledged before me on _____, 20___, by MARY M. DOE, *as Trustee, who is personally known to me or who has produced adequate identification.*

_____
Notary Public

Appendix B: Some Additional Clauses

The following are additional clauses that may be used in addition to or in lieu of clauses in the sample trust agreement.

Life Estate Clause

The law with respect to creating a life use is different in every state and should be reviewed carefully if that is the grantor's intention. Generally, the common law, or in some cases statutory law, will identify the respective rights and obligations of the life tenant and remaindermen, including care and use of the property. Regardless of how well defined the law is, it is preferable to set forth those terms within the clause establishing the life tenancy. In many cases, it is simply easier to create a trust rather than a life use in real estate. Where a life estate is desired, the following language may be used.

> *I give my wife (hereafter the "life tenant") the right to use and occupy my residence at 123 Main Street, Anytown, Anystate for her lifetime. Upon the death of the life tenant, such property shall be distributed to my then-living descendant, per stirpes (hereafter the "remaindermen"). The life tenant shall be responsible for all ordinary maintenance of the property, all necessary capital improvements, obtaining adequate casualty insurance, real estate taxes and other assessment. The life tenant shall be entitled to all rental receipts. In the event of loss of the property due to condemnation, fire or other casualty, the decision to restore the property shall be made in the sole discretion of the life tenant. If the life tenant declines to restore the property, the value of any insurance proceeds shall be divided between the life tenant and the remaindermen based on the proportionate interests of each based on the actuarial life expectancy of the life tenant as would be determined for federal estate tax purposes as if the life estate was created on the date of loss.*

Many of the provisions in this clause may be contrary to the default provisions under state law. Typically, capital improvements would be borne by the remaindermen. Also, the treatment of insurance proceeds and the right to elect to restore the property may be very different under state law. The decision to include some or all of these provisions should be considered in light of the grantor's objectives. In all events, however, it is preferable to spell out the relative rights and responsibilities of the parties rather than leaving the question to be determined under the prevailing state law.

Pet Disposition Clause

When the grantor desires to make special provisions for the disposition of his pets, the following language may be used.

> ***Bequest of Pet.*** *I give my dog, Fifi, or any other pet I own at my death, to my cousin, Vincent Roe, if he survives me. My Trustees shall incur all reasonable expenses of caring for my pet prior to delivery and for transporting my pet to my cousin. In addition, I give the sum of One Thousand Dollars ($1,000) to my cousin, Vincent Roe, if he survives me and if he accepts care and custody of my pet. It is my request, without creating a legal obligation, that my cousin use such amount to provide for the comfortable care of my pet.*

When the grantor has specific wishes regarding a pet, it is important to set forth those wishes either in a will or the revocable trust. It is important to consult the proposed taker of the pet and receive his or her agreement to accept the pet before naming him. Even if the named taker agrees, it is wise to include an alternate taker in the event that circumstances change and the named taker cannot accept the pet. The clause can refer to the current pet by name, but as a practical matter it also should refer to any future pet as well. The cost of caring for and transporting the pet to the taker should be borne by the estate.

Some grantors also wish to provide a sum of money to the person who will care for the pet in order to help defray the costs of caring for the pet and to ensure that the pet will have comfortable care. The cash bequest should be given directly to the taker with a request that it be used for the pet, and not

Appendix B: Some Additional Clauses

directly to the pet. While it is possible to establish pet trusts in some states, the requirements to do so are very specific. Section 408 of the Uniform Trust Code establishes the requirements for a valid pet trust and may be used as a guide even in states that have not yet adopted the code. A gift directly to the pet, or a mandate that the property be used only for the pet, may be void in states that do not recognize pet trusts, or where the terms do not qualify as a pet trust in those states that do permit them.

Alternate Distributions to Descendants

As indicated in the line-by-line analysis, there are a variety of options with respect to distributions to children. The first alternative option provides for an outright distribution to descendants, *per stirpes*. This option assumes an equal distribution among children. If an uneven distribution is preferred, the clause should be modified. Also, the clause assumes that the grantor is married and property will pass to the death of the survivor, thus the reference to "then-living descendants." If the grantor is not married and property will pass to descendants immediately at the death of the grantor, the phrase "my descendants who survive me, *per stirpes*" should be used instead.

Option One: Outright Distribution

> *Any property directed to be disposed of pursuant to this Article shall be distributed outright and free of trust to my then-living descendants, per stirpes.*

The second alternative option establishes a single trust for the benefit of all children until the youngest child reaches a specific age. This type of trust is appropriate where there are minor children and it is desirable to have adequate resources available to provide for the needs of the children, including education. The trustees can make distributions to each child according to need without requiring that the distributions be allocated against the share of a specific child. Ordinarily, the age will be such that the children will have the opportunity to complete at least college and, in some cases, graduate school, depending on the preference of the grantor. Thus reference to age twenty-two or twenty-five are both common options. Once the youngest child attains the specified age, the single trust terminates and separate trusts are established for each child as under the terms of Article VI in the sample trust agreement.

Option Two: Single Trust to Specified Age

Any property directed to be disposed of pursuant to this Article shall be disposed of as follows:

(A) **Single Trust for Descendents.** *Such property shall be held in a single trust until my youngest living child attains the age of twenty-five (25) years. During the continuance of such trust, the Trustees may distribute so much or all of the net income and principal of such trust to such one or more members of the class of individuals consisting of my descendants who are living from time to time during the term of the trust, in such shares and proportions, without requirement of equality, as the Trustees consider advisable to provide for the education, maintenance in health and reasonable comfort, and support in accustomed manner of living of any one or more of such individuals. In addition, the Independent Trustee may distribute so much or all of the net income and principal thereof to such one or more members of such class, in such shares and proportions, without requirement of equality, as the Independent Trustee considers advisable in its sole, absolute and uncontrolled discretion for any purposes whatsoever. The Trustees shall accumulate and add to principal at least annually any net income not so paid.*

(B) **Termination of Single Trust.** *At such time as my youngest living child attains the age of twenty-five (25) years, the remaining trust property shall be divided into separate shares, per stirpes, with respect to my then living descendants, and such shares shall be disposed of as follows:*

[continuing trust as under Article VI of the sample trust, or outright distribution as noted in Option 1 above]

ABOUT THE AUTHOR

Kelley Galica Peck, JD, LLM, is the chair of the Trusts & Estates Practice Group at the Hartford, Connecticut-based law firm of Halloran & Sage LLP. For more than a decade, her practice has been dedicated exclusively to complex and sophisticated estate planning. Ms. Peck is also an adjunct professor of law in the Master of Laws (LLM) program in Estate Planning and Elder Law at Western New England School of Law in Springfield, Massachusetts, teaching advanced legal courses in drafting wills and trusts and tax planning for the marital deduction.